Steve Niles' C
of Unspeakal

ALEISTER ARCANE™

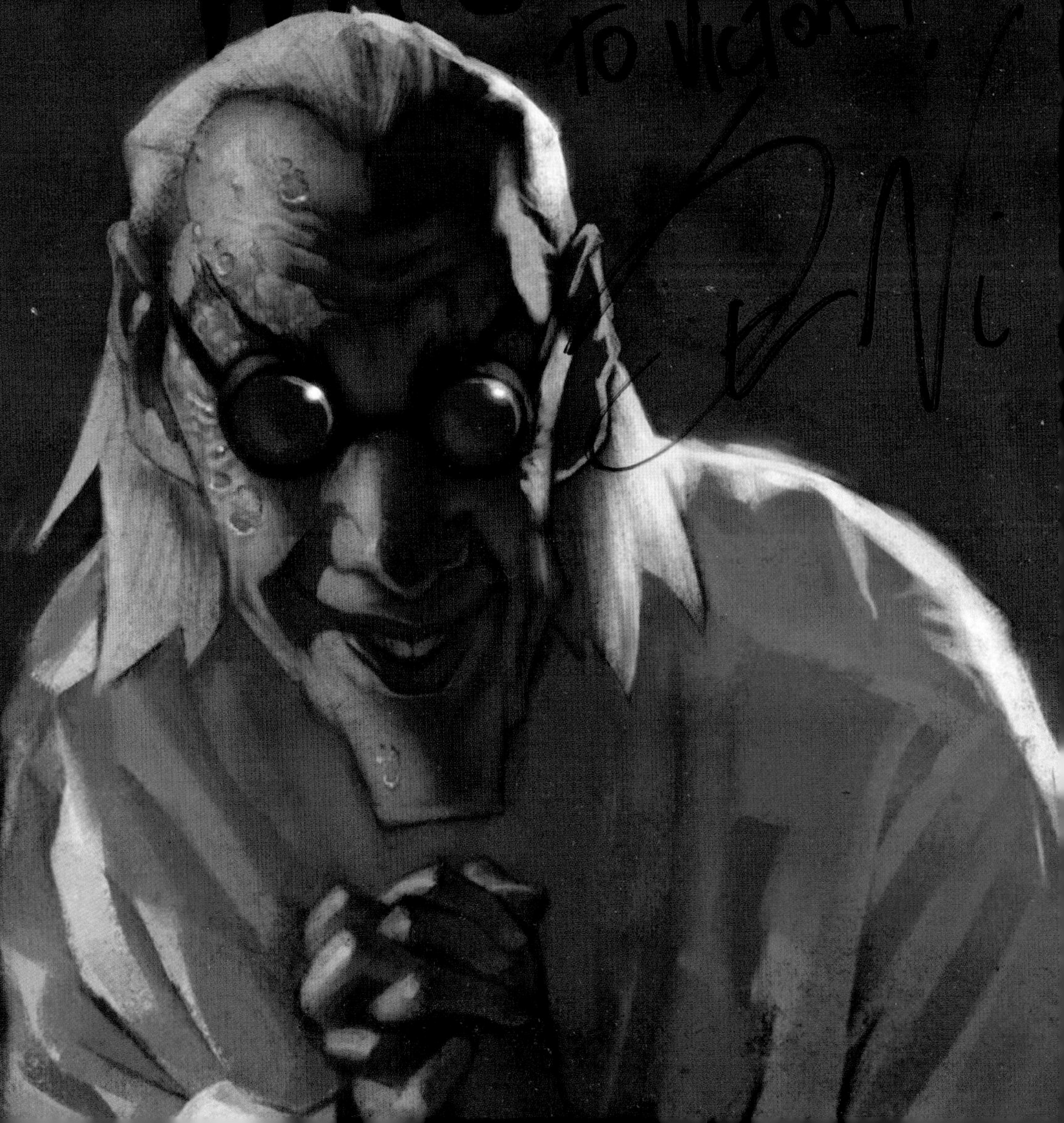
To Victor!

Become our fan on Facebook **facebook.com/idwpublishing**
Follow us on Twitter **@idwpublishing**

Subscribe to us on YouTube **youtube.com/idwpublishing**
See what's new on Tumblr **tumblr.idwpublishing.com**
Check us out on Instagram **instagram.com/idwpublsing**

ISBN: 978-1-63140-828-1   19 18 '17 16 1 2 3 4

Originally published as ALEISTER ARCANE issues #1–3.

Ted Adams, CEO & Publisher
Greg Goldstein, President & COO
Robbie Robbins, EVP/Sr. Graphic Artist
Chris Ryall, Chief Creative Officer/Editor-in-Chief
Laurie Windrow, Senior Vice President of Sales & Marketing
Matthew Ruzicka, CPA, Chief Financial Officer
Dirk Wood, VP of Marketing
Lorelei Bunjes, VP of Digital Services
Jeff Webber, VP of Licensing, Digital and Subsidiary Rights
Jerry Bennington, VP of New Product Development

Written by
Steve Niles

Art and Lettering by
Breehn Burns

Series Edits by
Jeff Mariotte

Cover Art by
Sam Shearon

Collection Edits by
Justin Eisinger and **Alonzo Simon**

Collection Design by
Ron Estevez

Publisher
Ted Adams

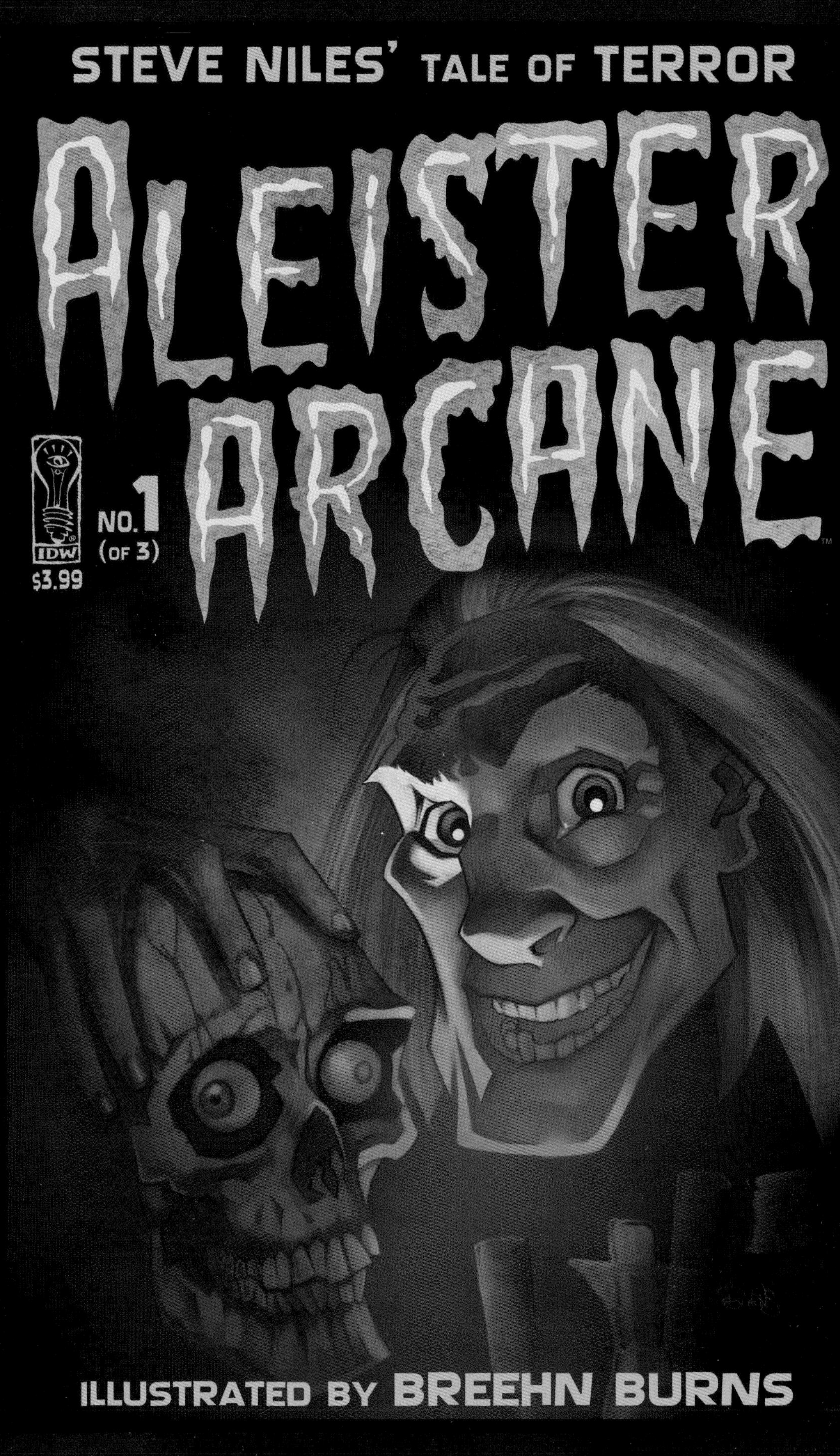
STEVE NILES' TALE OF TERROR
ALEISTER ARCANE™
IDW
NO. 1 (OF 3)
$3.99
ILLUSTRATED BY BREEHN BURNS

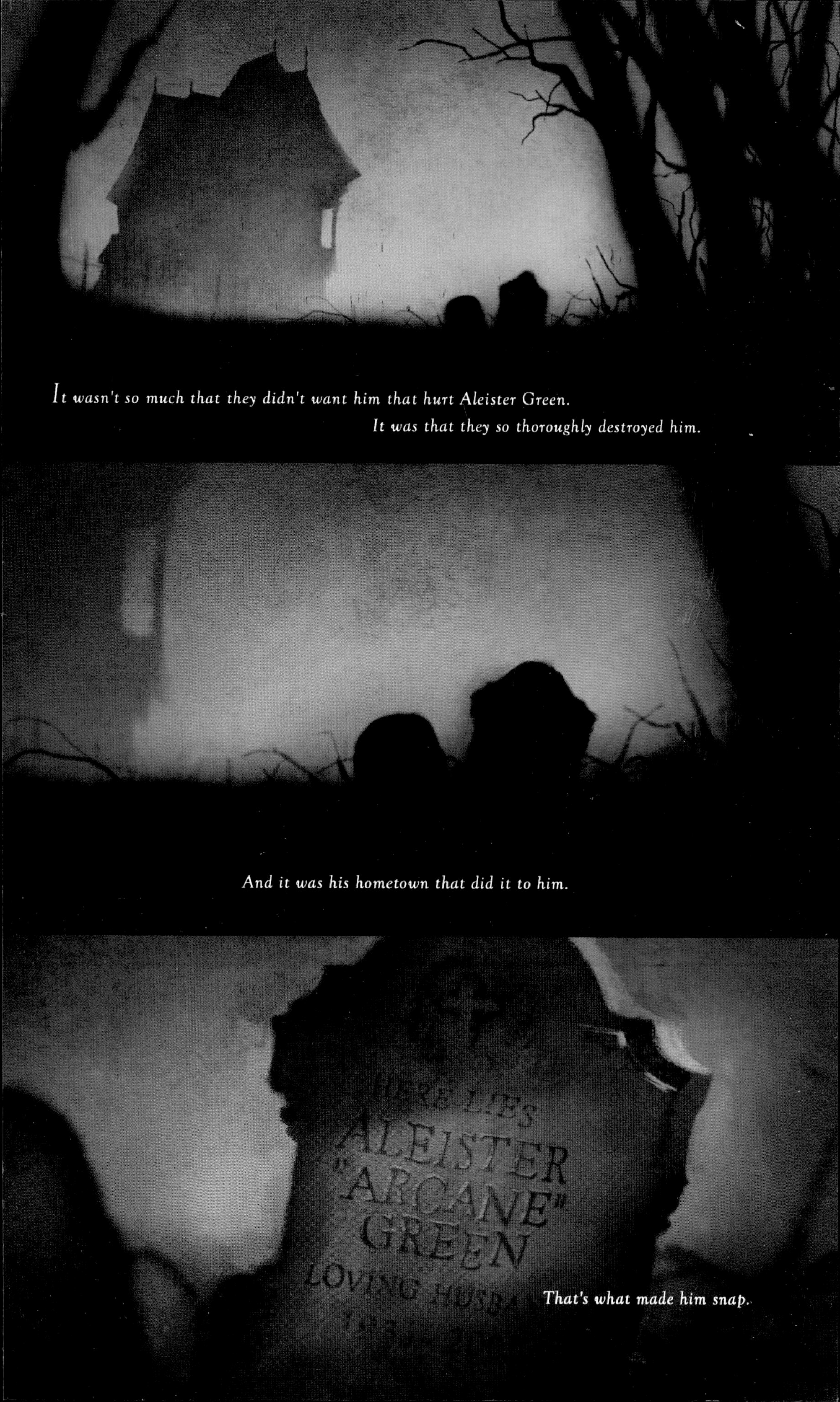
It wasn't so much that they didn't want him that hurt Aleister Green.
It was that they so thoroughly destroyed him.
And it was his hometown that did it to him.
HERE LIES
ALEISTER
"ARCANE"
GREEN
That's what made him snap.

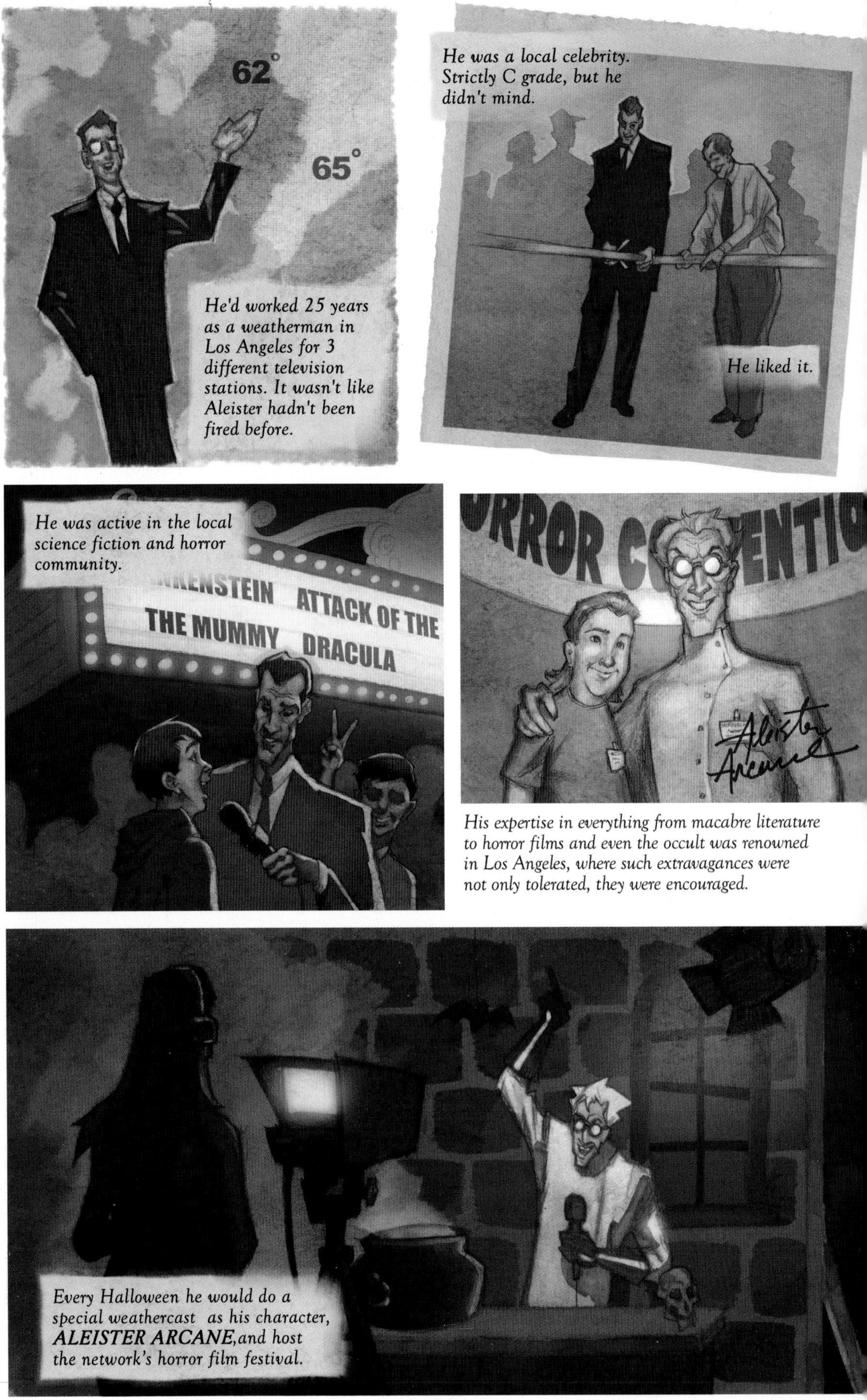
62°
65°
He'd worked 25 years as a weatherman in Los Angeles for 3 different television stations. It wasn't like Aleister hadn't been fired before.
He was a local celebrity. Strictly C grade, but he didn't mind.
He liked it.
He was active in the local science fiction and horror community.
ATTACK OF THE
THE MUMMY
DRACULA
Aleister Arcane
His expertise in everything from macabre literature to horror films and even the occult was renowned in Los Angeles, where such extravagances were not only tolerated, they were encouraged.
Every Halloween he would do a special weathercast as his character, ALEISTER ARCANE, and host the network's horror film festival.

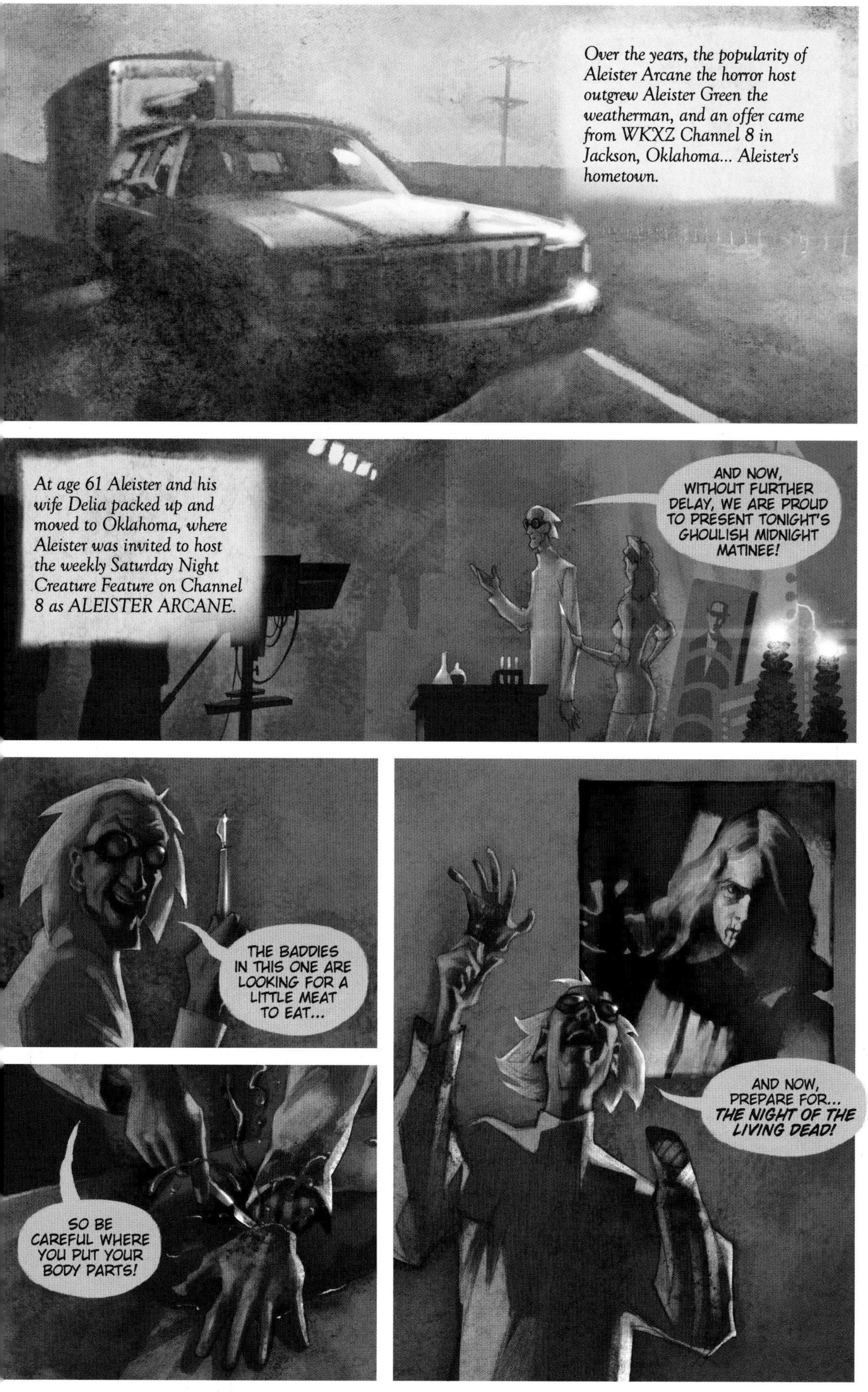
Over the years, the popularity of Aleister Arcane the horror host outgrew Aleister Green the weatherman, and an offer came from WKXZ Channel 8 in Jackson, Oklahoma... Aleister's hometown.
At age 61 Aleister and his wife Delia packed up and moved to Oklahoma, where Aleister was invited to host the weekly Saturday Night Creature Feature on Channel 8 as ALEISTER ARCANE.
AND NOW, WITHOUT FURTHER DELAY, WE ARE PROUD TO PRESENT TONIGHT'S GHOULISH MIDNIGHT MATINEE!
THE BADDIES IN THIS ONE ARE LOOKING FOR A LITTLE MEAT TO EAT...
SO BE CAREFUL WHERE YOU PUT YOUR BODY PARTS!
AND NOW, PREPARE FOR... THE NIGHT OF THE LIVING DEAD!

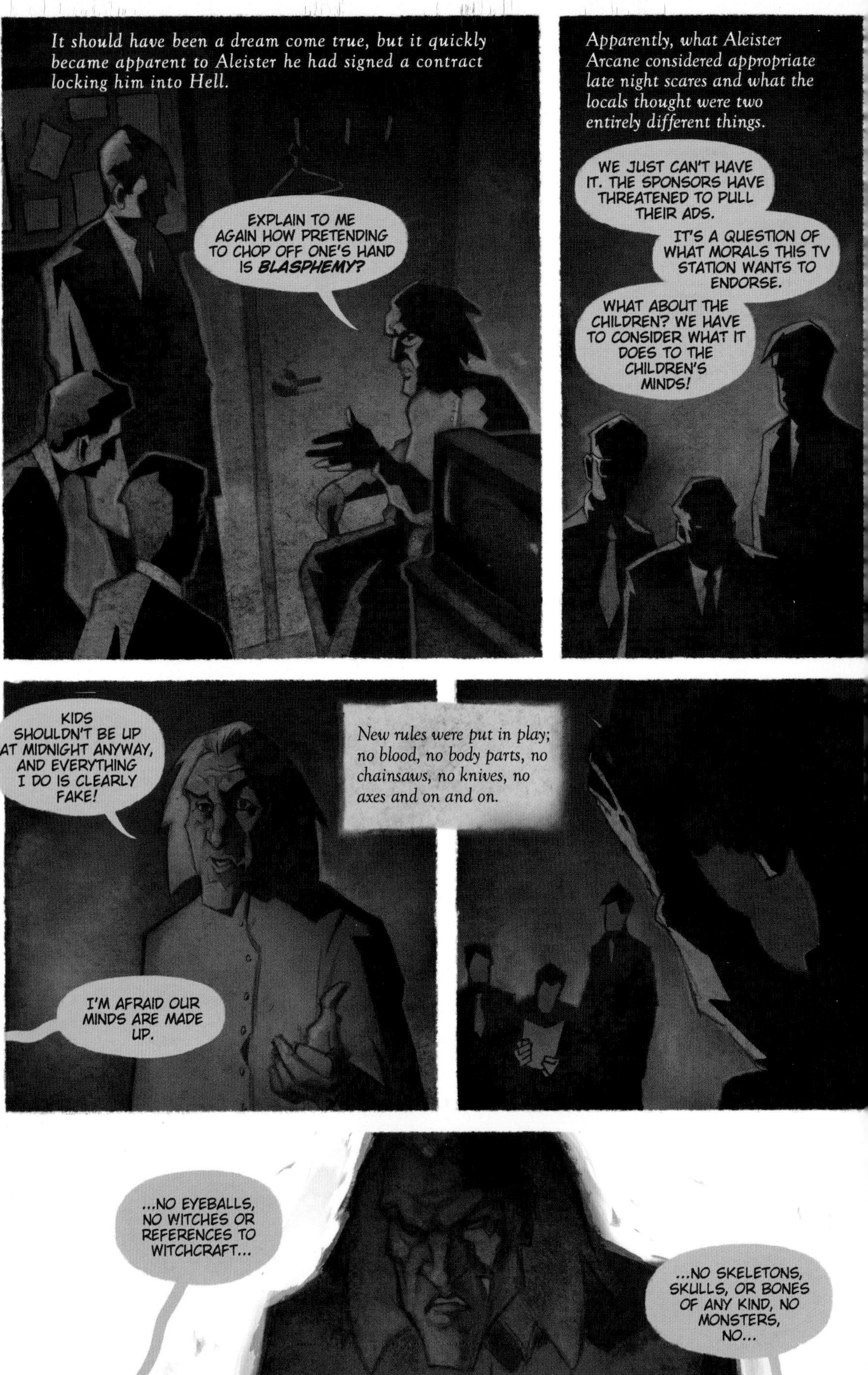
It should have been a dream come true, but it quickly became apparent to Aleister he had signed a contract locking him into Hell.
EXPLAIN TO ME AGAIN HOW PRETENDING TO CHOP OFF ONE'S HAND IS BLASPHEMY?
Apparently, what Aleister Arcane considered appropriate late night scares and what the locals thought were two entirely different things.
WE JUST CAN'T HAVE IT. THE SPONSORS HAVE THREATENED TO PULL THEIR ADS.
IT'S A QUESTION OF WHAT MORALS THIS TV STATION WANTS TO ENDORSE.
WHAT ABOUT THE CHILDREN? WE HAVE TO CONSIDER WHAT IT DOES TO THE CHILDREN'S MINDS!
KIDS SHOULDN'T BE UP AT MIDNIGHT ANYWAY, AND EVERYTHING I DO IS CLEARLY FAKE!
I'M AFRAID OUR MINDS ARE MADE UP.
New rules were put in play; no blood, no body parts, no chainsaws, no knives, no axes and on and on.
...NO EYEBALLS, NO WITCHES OR REFERENCES TO WITCHCRAFT...
...NO SKELETONS, SKULLS, OR BONES OF ANY KIND, NO MONSTERS, NO...

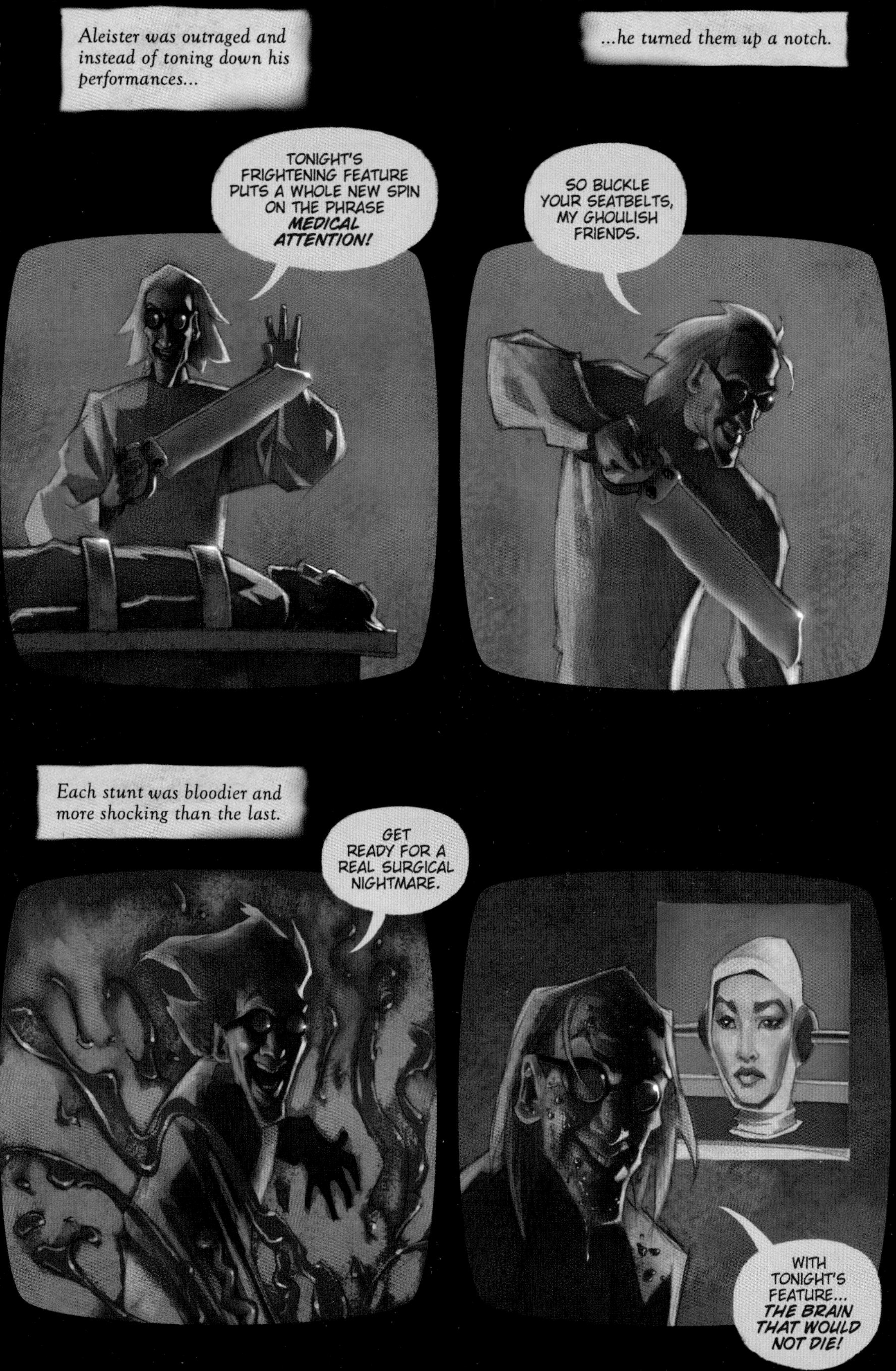
Aleister was outraged and instead of toning down his performances...
...he turned them up a notch.
TONIGHT'S FRIGHTENING FEATURE PUTS A WHOLE NEW SPIN ON THE PHRASE MEDICAL ATTENTION!
SO BUCKLE YOUR SEATBELTS, MY GHOULISH FRIENDS.
Each stunt was bloodier and more shocking than the last.
GET READY FOR A REAL SURGICAL NIGHTMARE.
WITH TONIGHT'S FEATURE... THE BRAIN THAT WOULD NOT DIE!

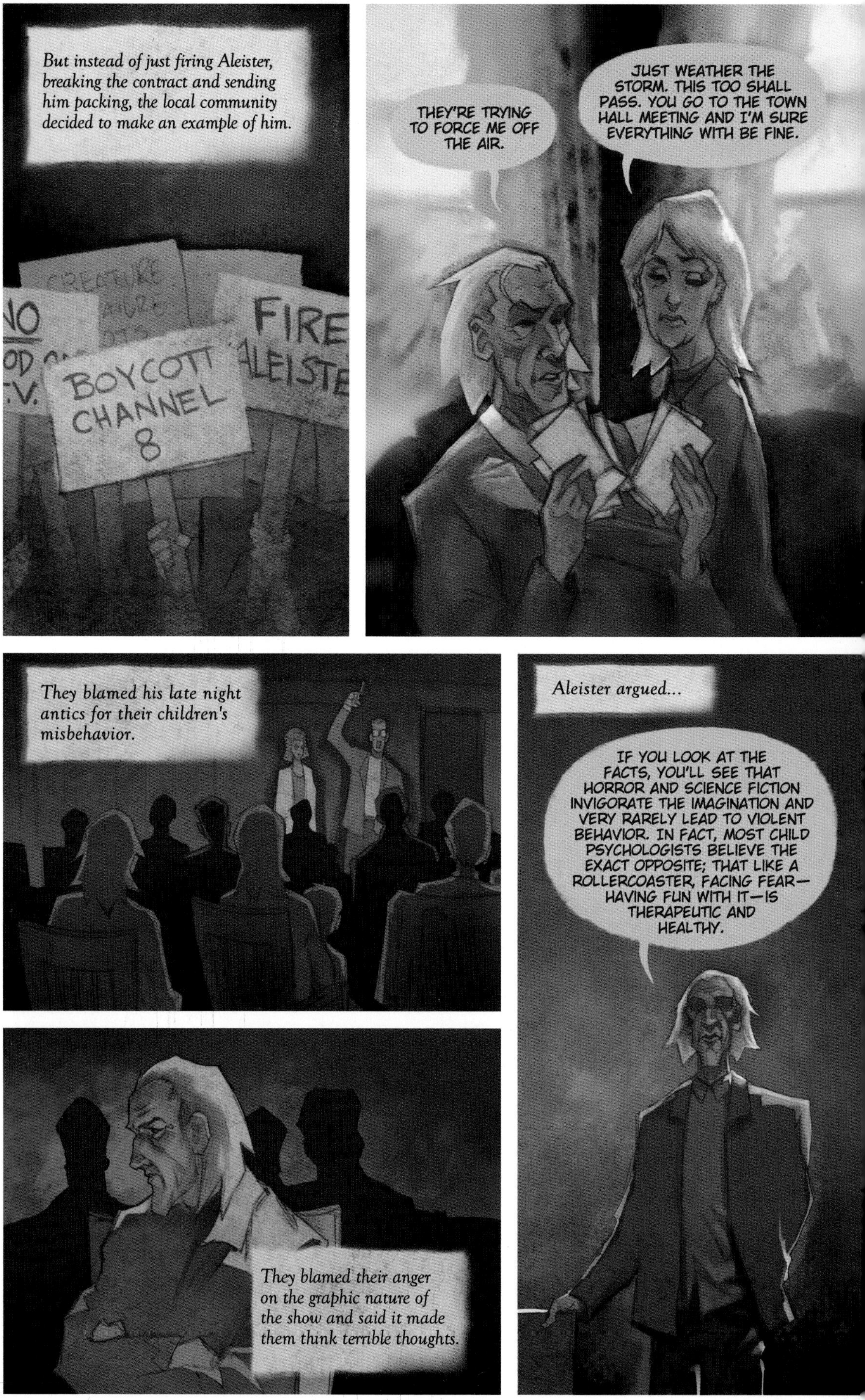

But instead of just firing Aleister, breaking the contract and sending him packing, the local community decided to make an example of him.
NO
BOYCOTT CHANNEL 8
FIRE
THEY'RE TRYING TO FORCE ME OFF THE AIR.
JUST WEATHER THE STORM. THIS TOO SHALL PASS. YOU GO TO THE TOWN HALL MEETING AND I'M SURE EVERYTHING WITH BE FINE.
They blamed his late night antics for their children's misbehavior.
They blamed their anger on the graphic nature of the show and said it made them think terrible thoughts.
Aleister argued...
IF YOU LOOK AT THE FACTS, YOU'LL SEE THAT HORROR AND SCIENCE FICTION INVIGORATE THE IMAGINATION AND VERY RARELY LEAD TO VIOLENT BEHAVIOR. IN FACT, MOST CHILD PSYCHOLOGISTS BELIEVE THE EXACT OPPOSITE; THAT LIKE A ROLLERCOASTER, FACING FEAR—HAVING FUN WITH IT—IS THERAPEUTIC AND HEALTHY.

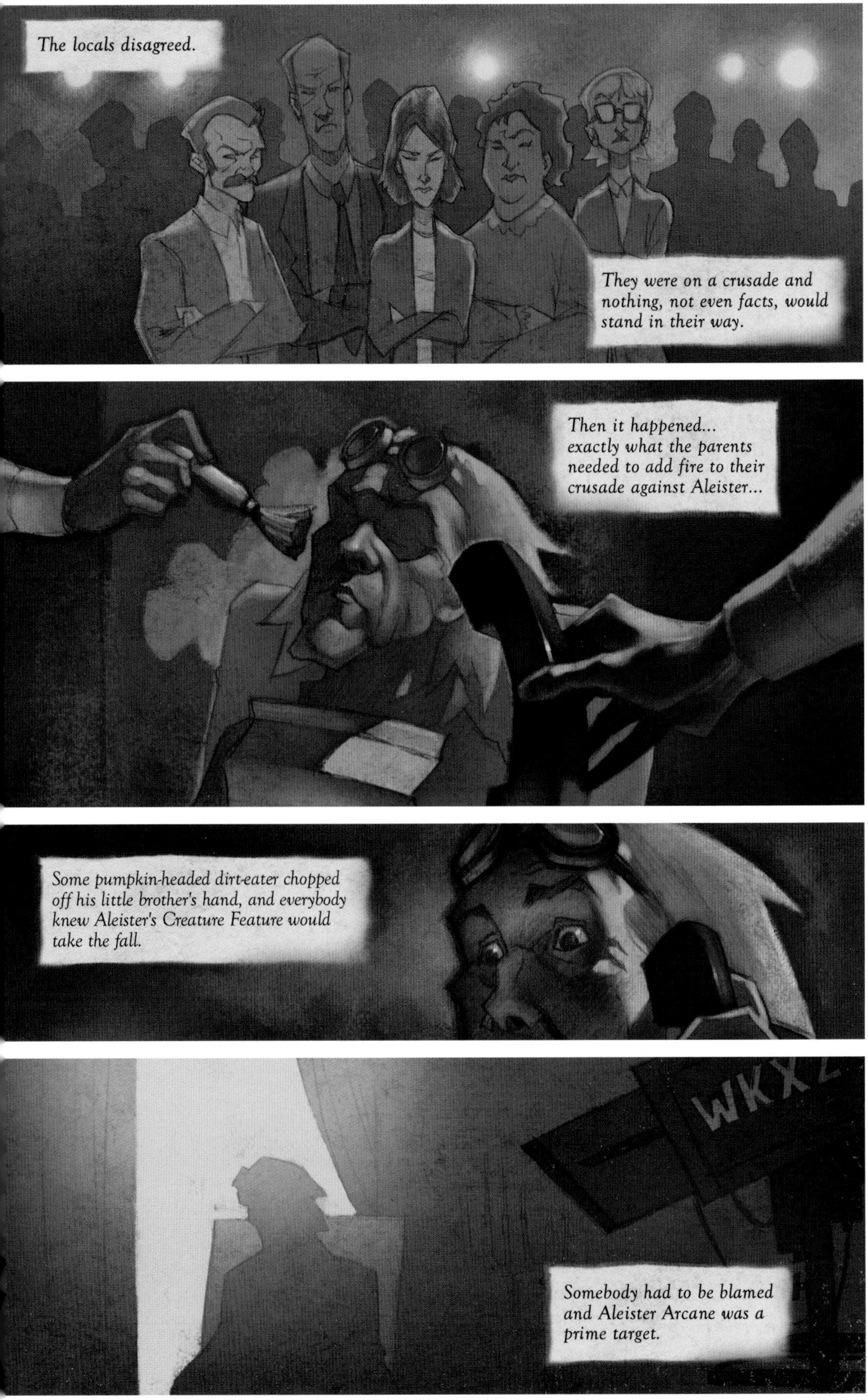
The locals disagreed.
They were on a crusade and nothing, not even facts, would stand in their way.
Then it happened... exactly what the parents needed to add fire to their crusade against Aleister...
Some pumpkin-headed dirt-eater chopped off his little brother's hand, and everybody knew Aleister's Creature Feature would take the fall.
WKXZ
Somebody had to be blamed and Aleister Arcane was a prime target.

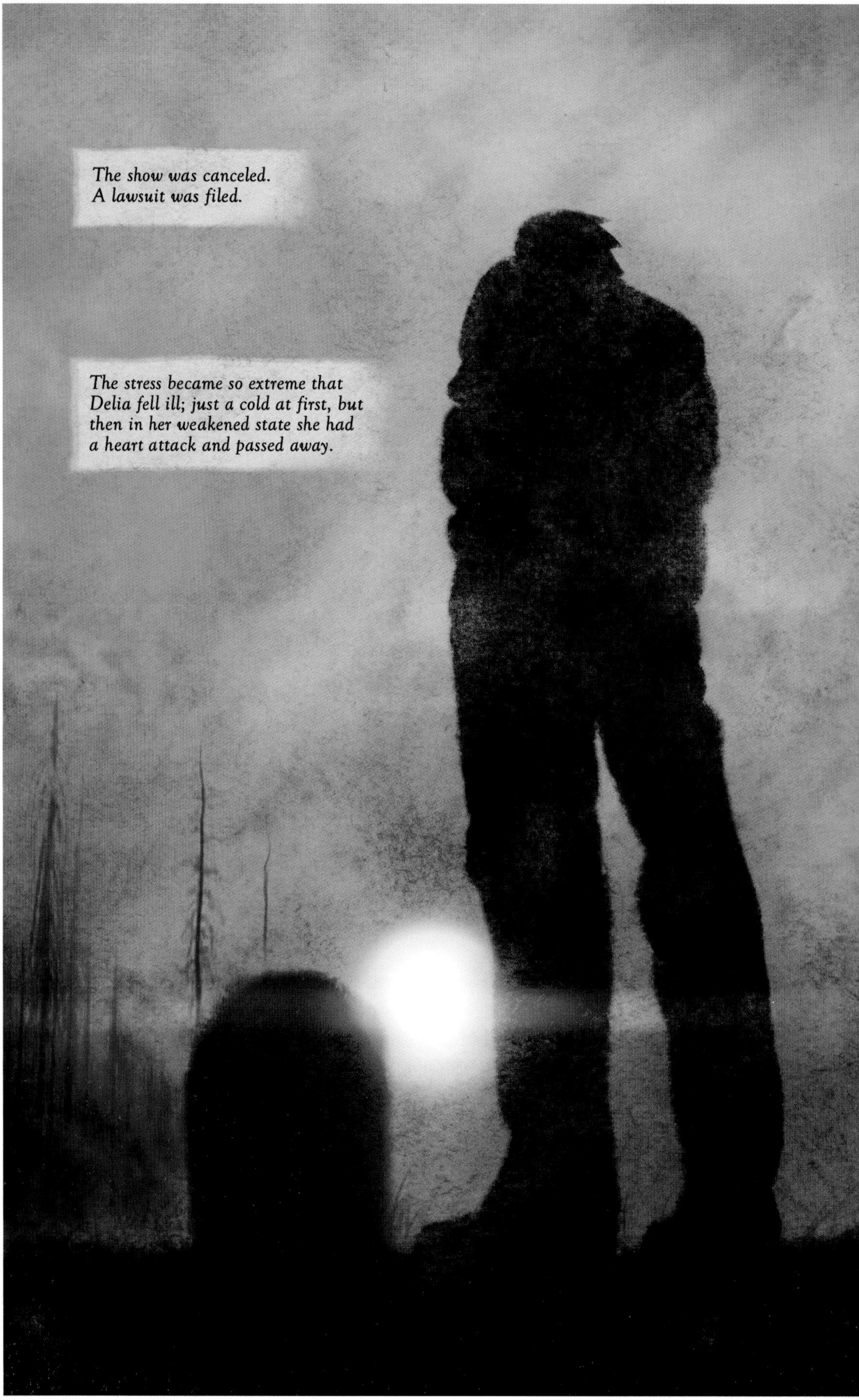
The show was canceled. A lawsuit was filed.
The stress became so extreme that Delia fell ill; just a cold at first, but then in her weakened state she had a heart attack and passed away.

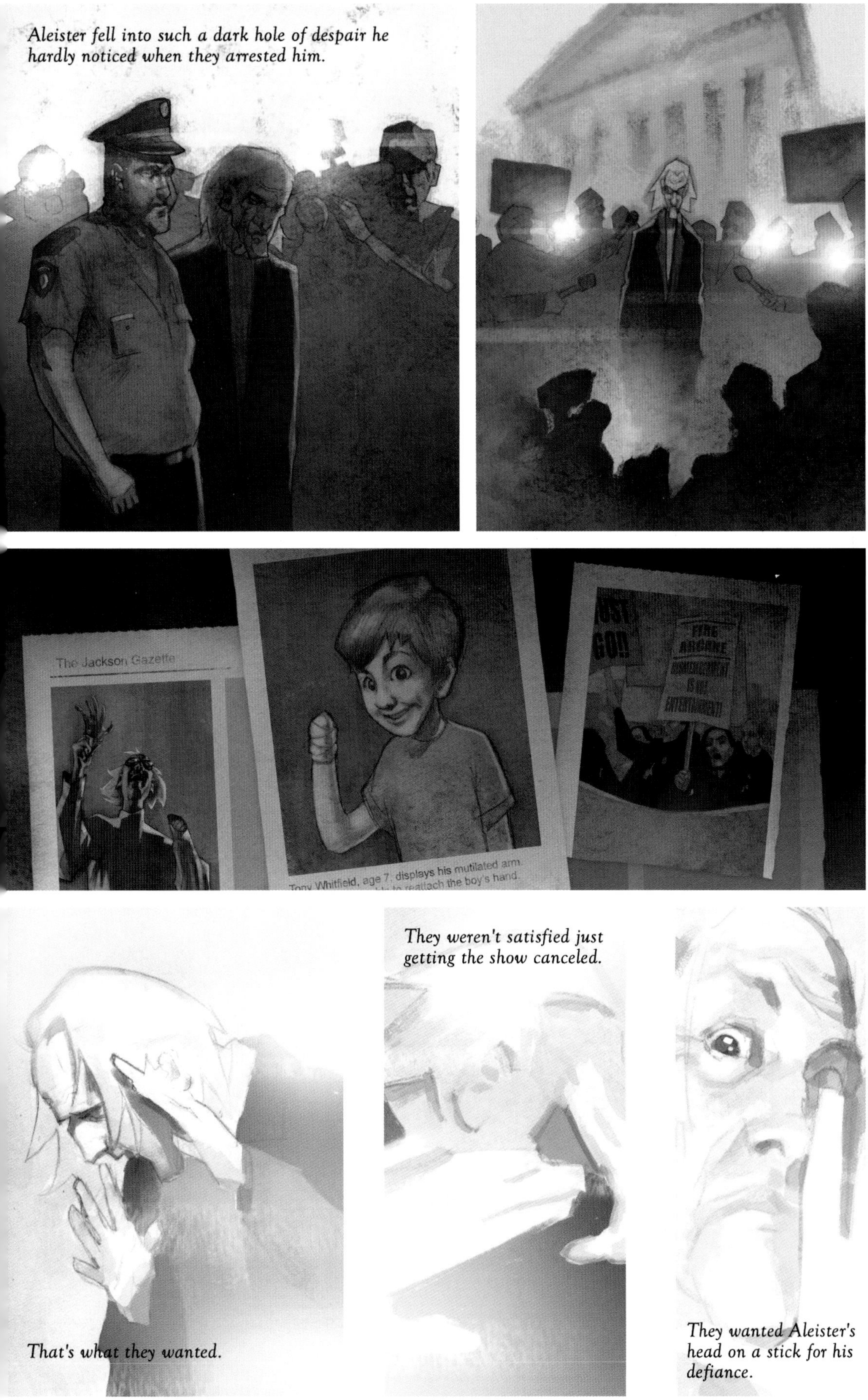
Aleister fell into such a dark hole of despair he hardly noticed when they arrested him.
The Jackson Gazette
Tony Whitfield, age 7, displays his mutilated arm.
That's what they wanted.
They weren't satisfied just getting the show canceled.
They wanted Aleister's head on a stick for his defiance.

It wasn't enough, so they blamed
him for their troubles. And finally,
when that wasn't enough, they
killed his beloved wife and dragged
him through the mud.

Aleister took it all with a stone face.
He sat through the trial and hardly
spoke a word, not even to his lawyer.

He wasn't convicted. The jury agreed
that Aleister's macabre pranks could
not cause a boy to hurt anyone.

Aleister was exonerated,
but he was ruined.

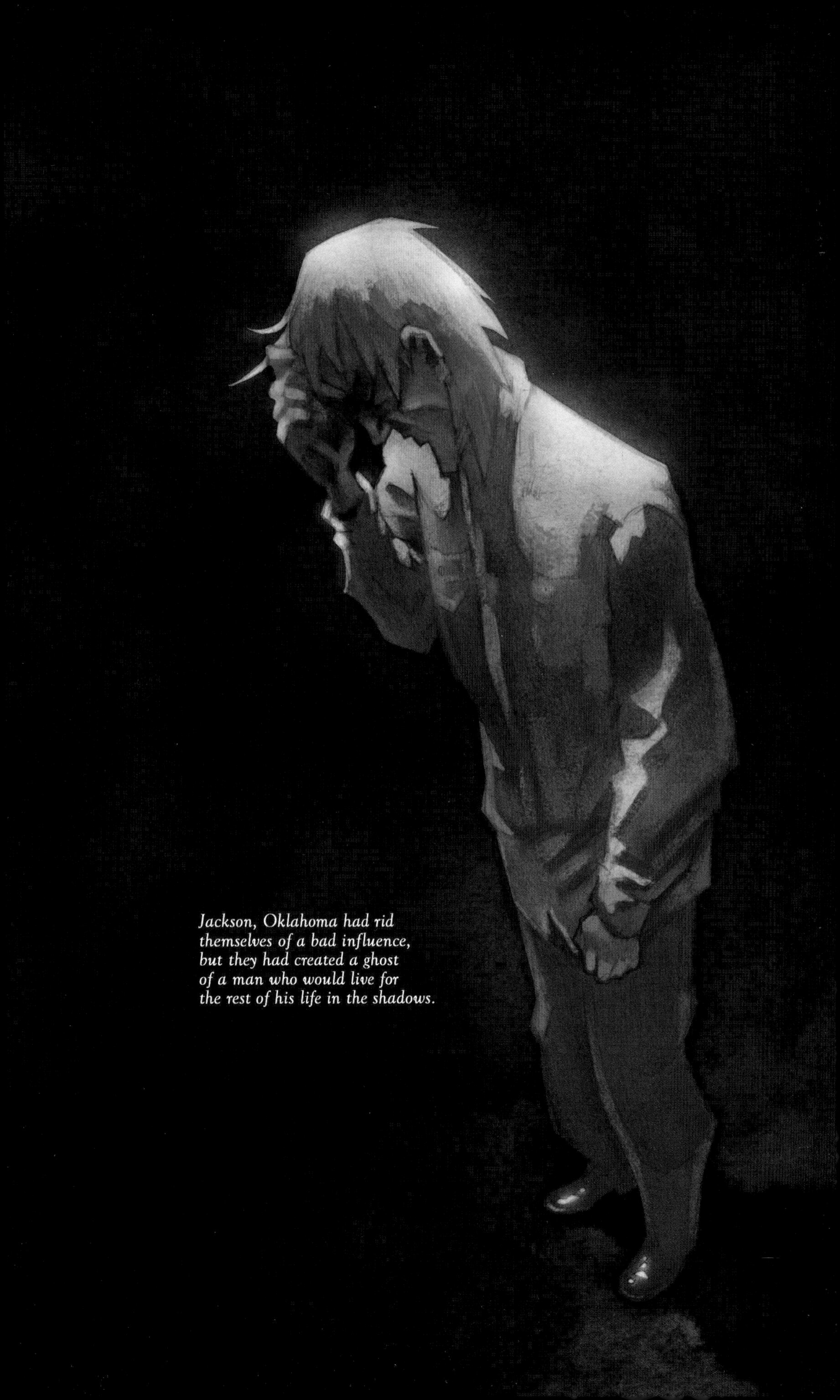
Jackson, Oklahoma had rid themselves of a bad influence, but they had created a ghost of a man who would live for the rest of his life in the shadows.

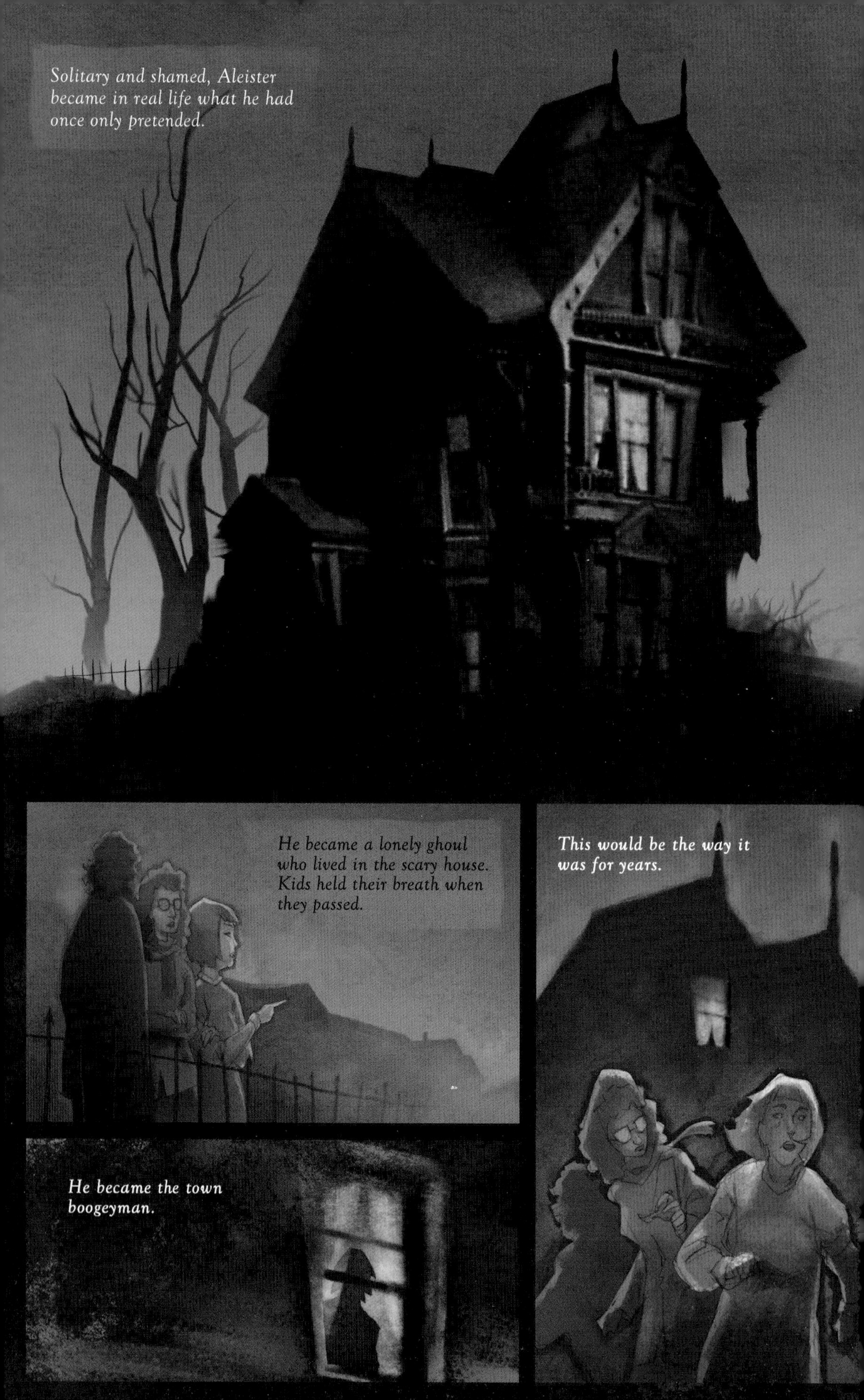
Solitary and shamed, Aleister became in real life what he had once only pretended.
He became a lonely ghoul who lived in the scary house. Kids held their breath when they passed.
He became the town boogeyman.
This would be the way it was for years.

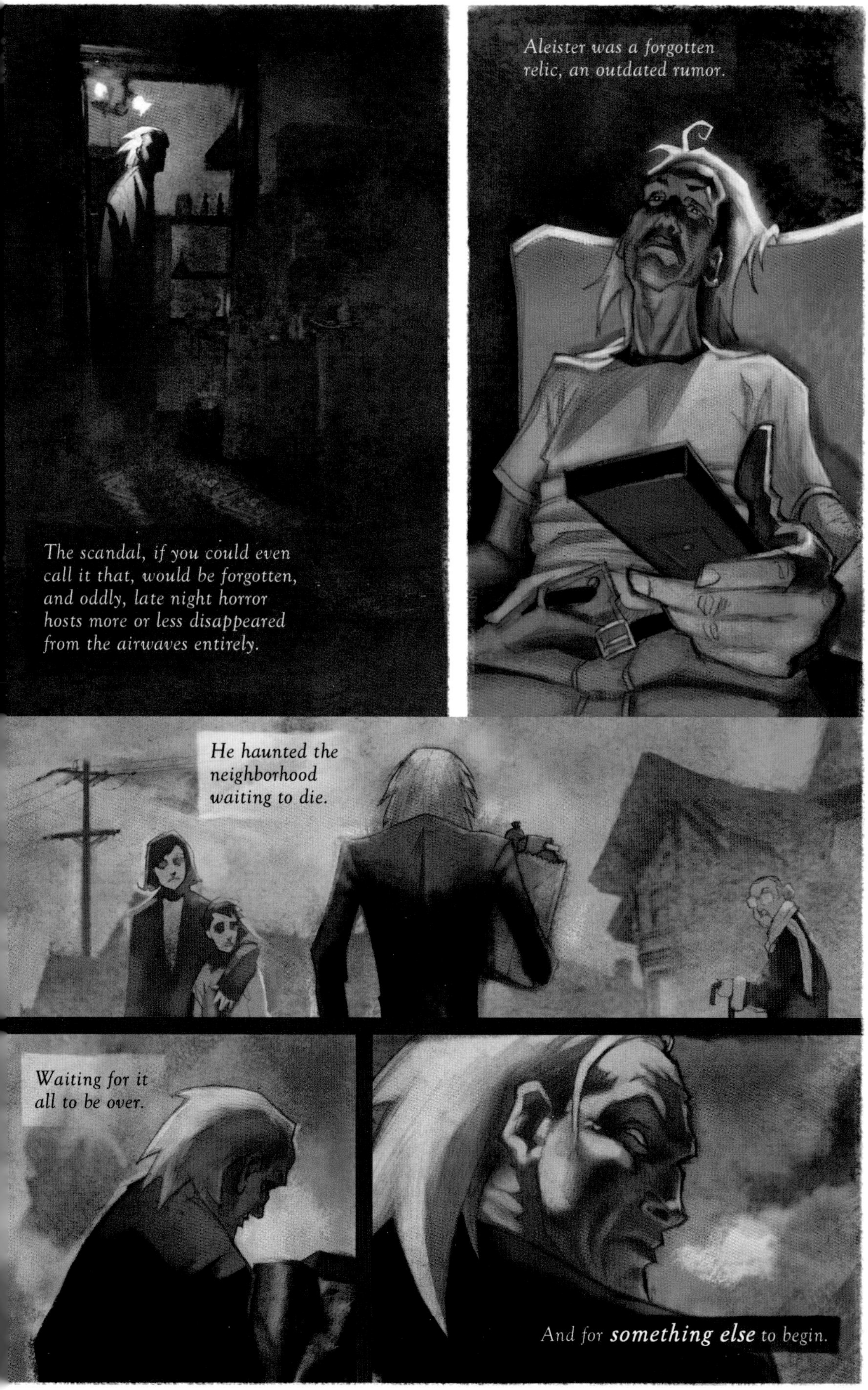
The scandal, if you could even call it that, would be forgotten, and oddly, late night horror hosts more or less disappeared from the airwaves entirely.
Aleister was a forgotten relic, an outdated rumor.
He haunted the neighborhood waiting to die.
Waiting for it all to be over.
And for **something else** to begin.

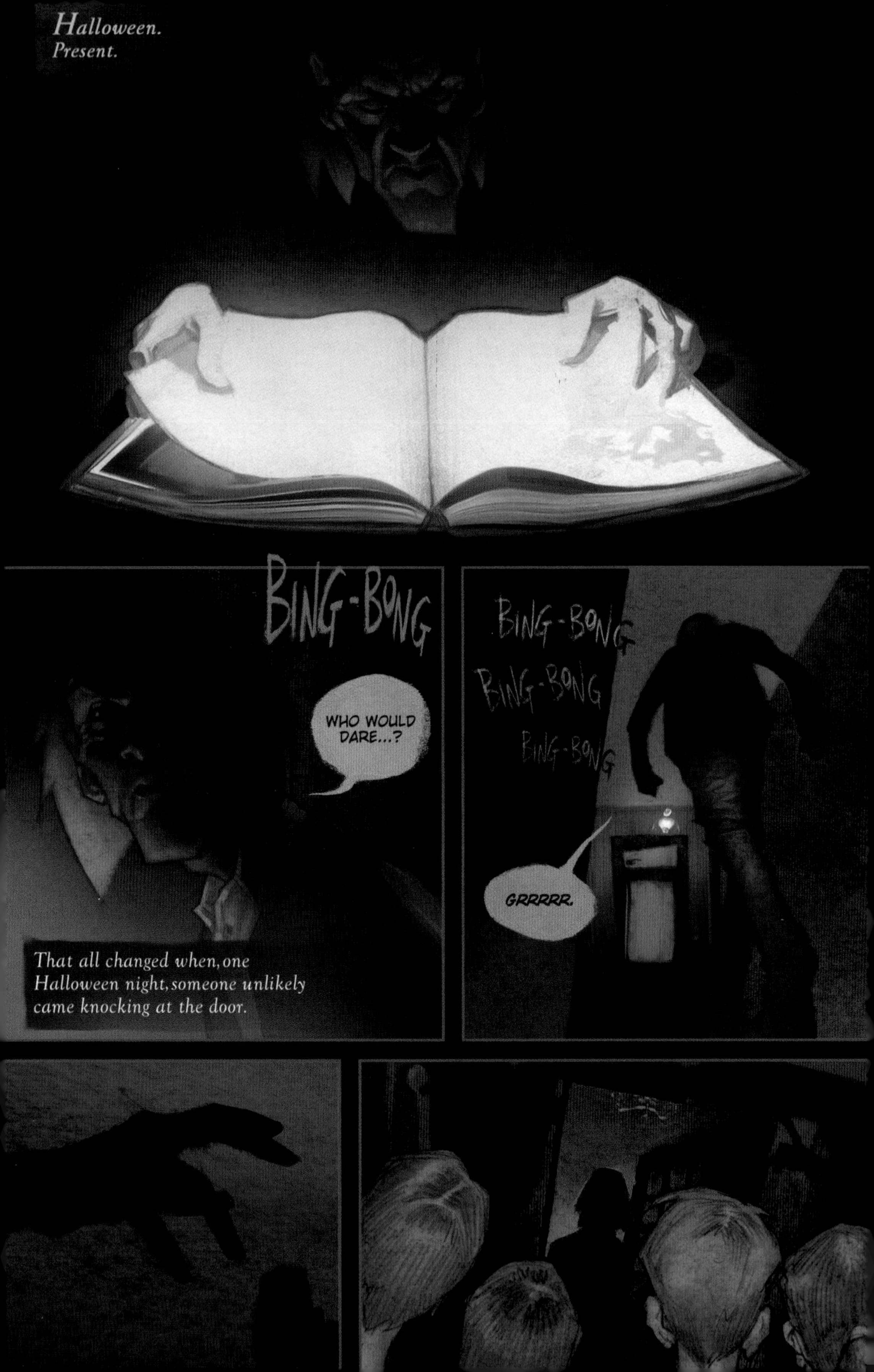
Halloween.
Present.
BING-BONG
WHO WOULD DARE...?
That all changed when, one Halloween night, someone unlikely came knocking at the door.
BING-BONG
BING-BONG
BING-BONG
GRRRRR.

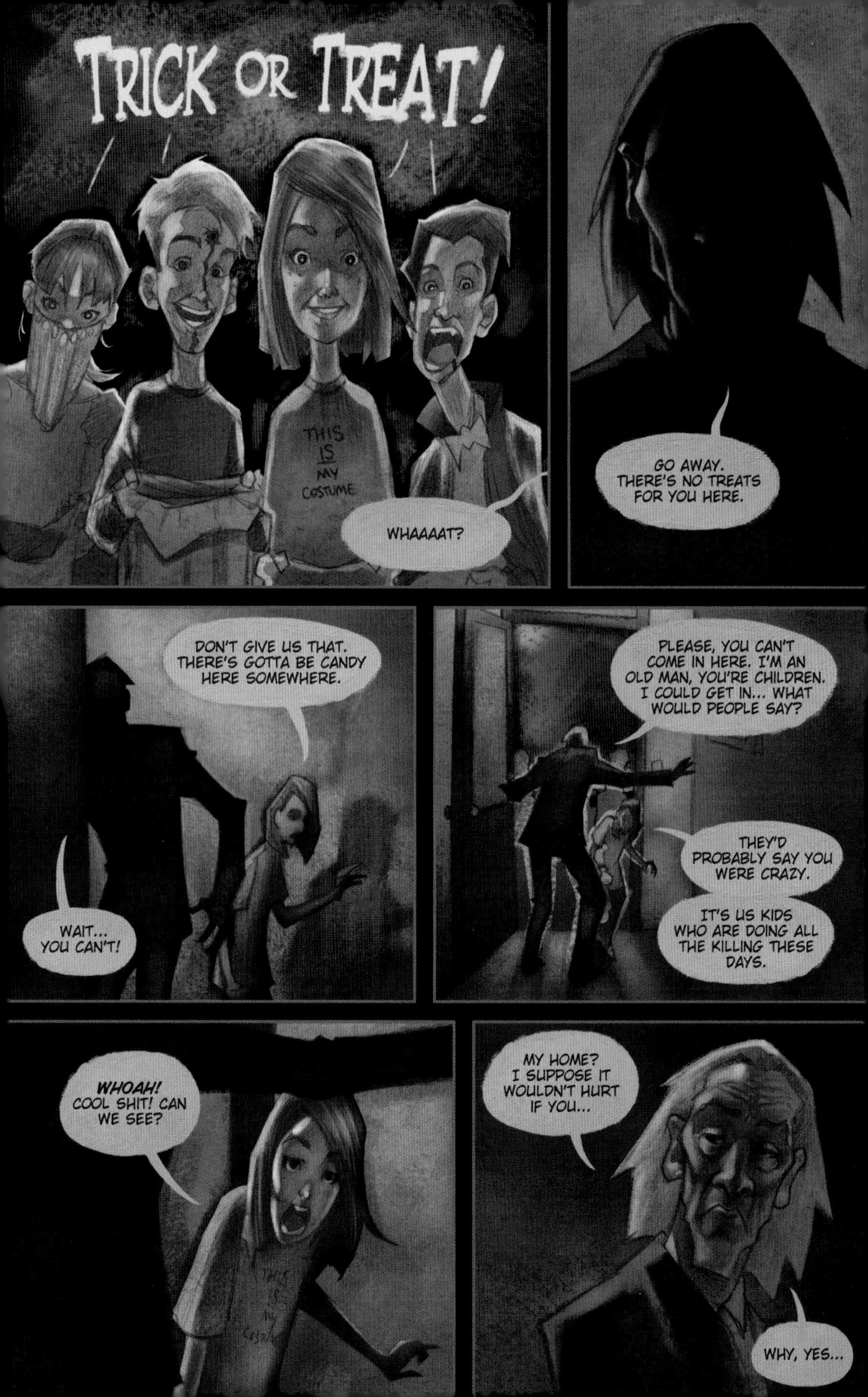
TRICK OR TREAT!
THIS IS MY COSTUME
WHAAAAT?
GO AWAY. THERE'S NO TREATS FOR YOU HERE.
DON'T GIVE US THAT. THERE'S GOTTA BE CANDY HERE SOMEWHERE.
WAIT... YOU CAN'T!
PLEASE, YOU CAN'T COME IN HERE. I'M AN OLD MAN, YOU'RE CHILDREN. I COULD GET IN... WHAT WOULD PEOPLE SAY?
THEY'D PROBABLY SAY YOU WERE CRAZY.
IT'S US KIDS WHO ARE DOING ALL THE KILLING THESE DAYS.
WHOAH! COOL SHIT! CAN WE SEE?
MY HOME? I SUPPOSE IT WOULDN'T HURT IF YOU...
WHY, YES...

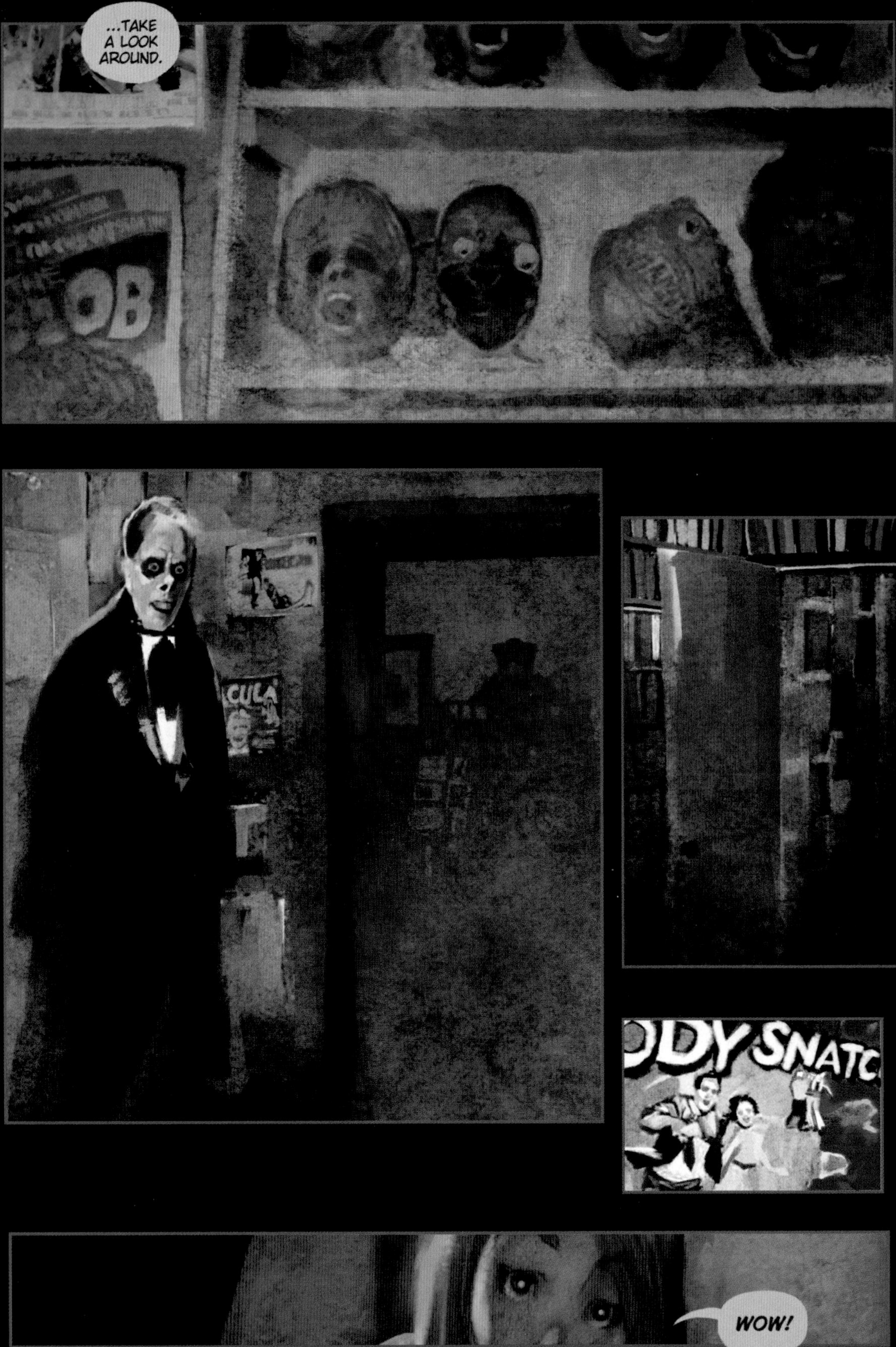
...TAKE A LOOK AROUND.
WOW!

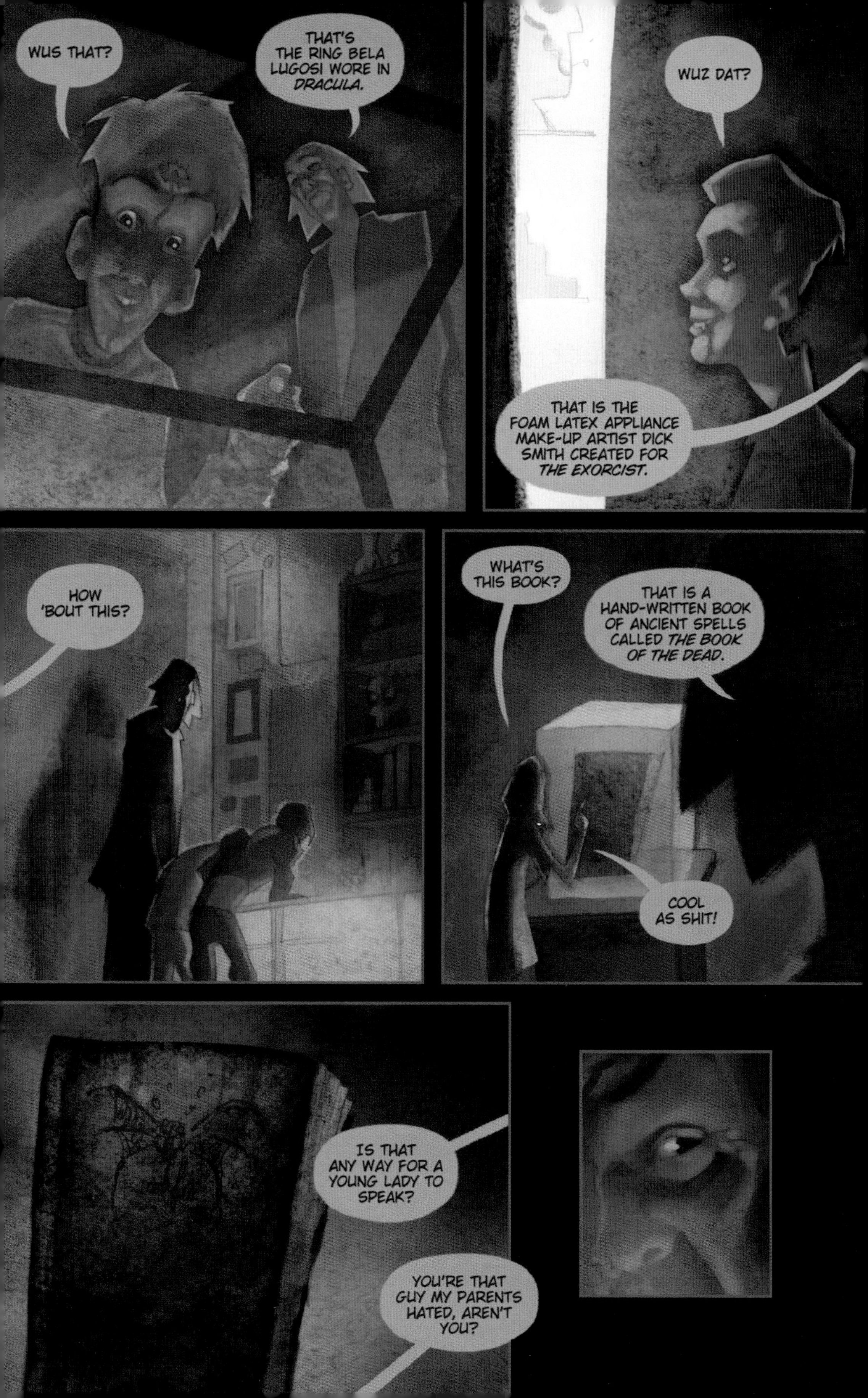
WUS THAT?
THAT'S THE RING BELA LUGOSI WORE IN *DRACULA.*
WUZ DAT?
THAT IS THE FOAM LATEX APPLIANCE MAKE-UP ARTIST DICK SMITH CREATED FOR *THE EXORCIST.*
HOW 'BOUT THIS?
WHAT'S THIS BOOK?
THAT IS A HAND-WRITTEN BOOK OF ANCIENT SPELLS CALLED *THE BOOK OF THE DEAD.*
COOL AS SHIT!
IS THAT ANY WAY FOR A YOUNG LADY TO SPEAK?
YOU'RE THAT GUY MY PARENTS HATED, AREN'T YOU?

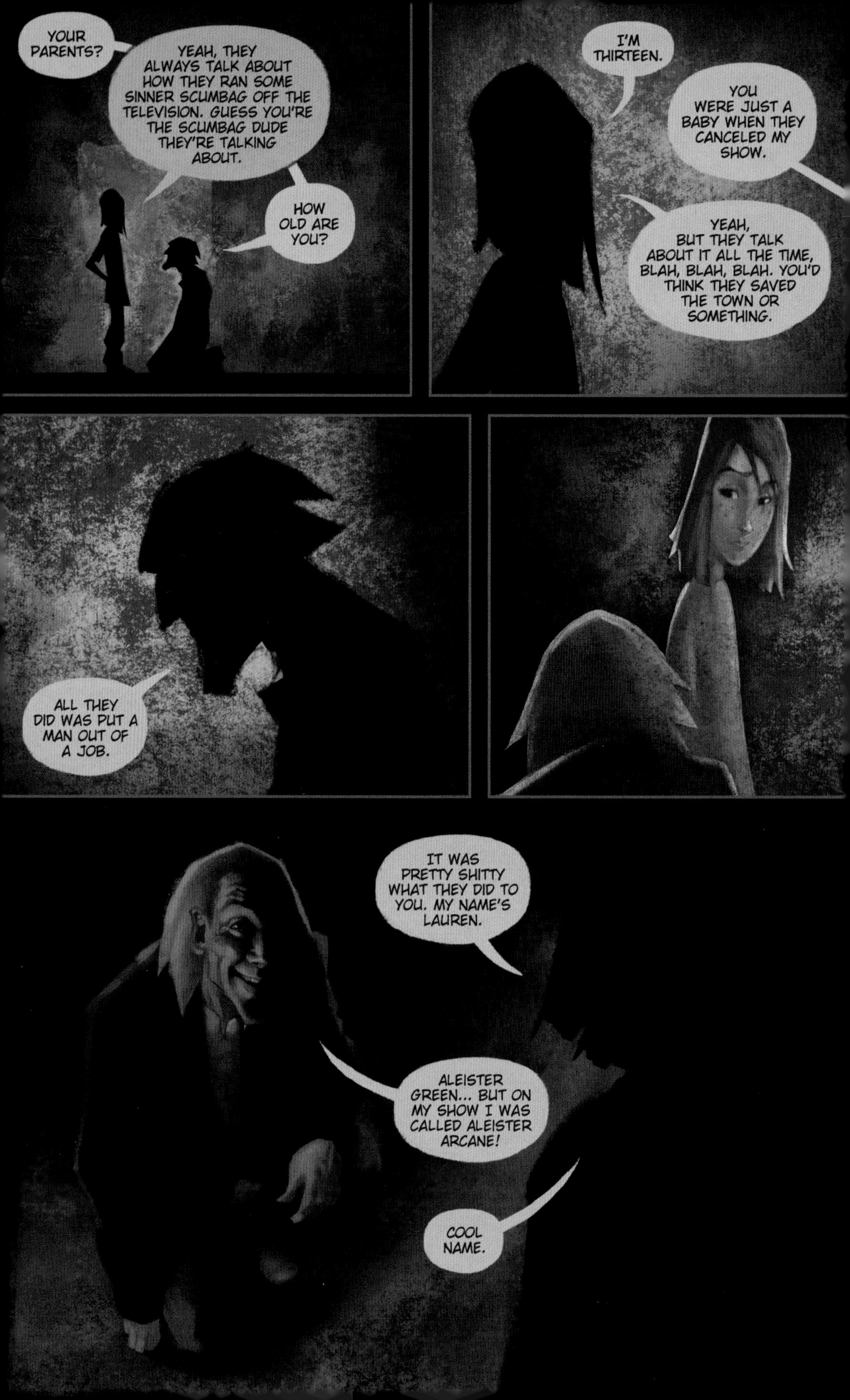
YOUR PARENTS?
YEAH, THEY ALWAYS TALK ABOUT HOW THEY RAN SOME SINNER SCUMBAG OFF THE TELEVISION. GUESS YOU'RE THE SCUMBAG DUDE THEY'RE TALKING ABOUT.
HOW OLD ARE YOU?
I'M THIRTEEN.
YOU WERE JUST A BABY WHEN THEY CANCELED MY SHOW.
YEAH, BUT THEY TALK ABOUT IT ALL THE TIME, BLAH, BLAH, BLAH. YOU'D THINK THEY SAVED THE TOWN OR SOMETHING.
ALL THEY DID WAS PUT A MAN OUT OF A JOB.
IT WAS PRETTY SHITTY WHAT THEY DID TO YOU. MY NAME'S LAUREN.
ALEISTER GREEN... BUT ON MY SHOW I WAS CALLED ALEISTER ARCANE!
COOL NAME.

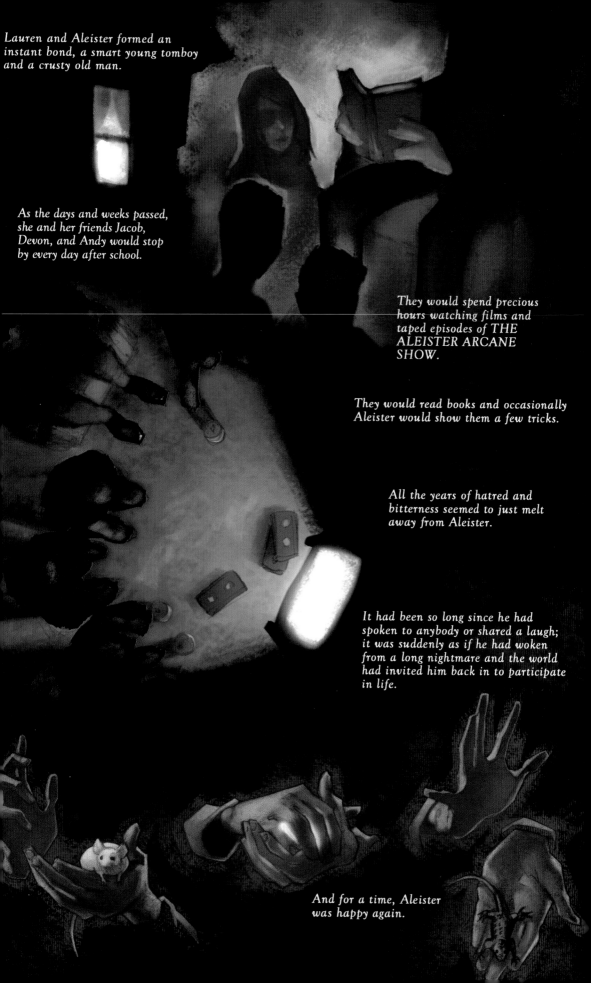

Lauren and Aleister formed an instant bond, a smart young tomboy and a crusty old man.

As the days and weeks passed, she and her friends Jacob, Devon, and Andy would stop by every day after school.

They would spend precious hours watching films and taped episodes of THE ALEISTER ARCANE SHOW.

They would read books and occasionally Aleister would show them a few tricks.

All the years of hatred and bitterness seemed to just melt away from Aleister.

It had been so long since he had spoken to anybody or shared a laugh; it was suddenly as if he had woken from a long nightmare and the world had invited him back in to participate in life.

And for a time, Aleister was happy again.

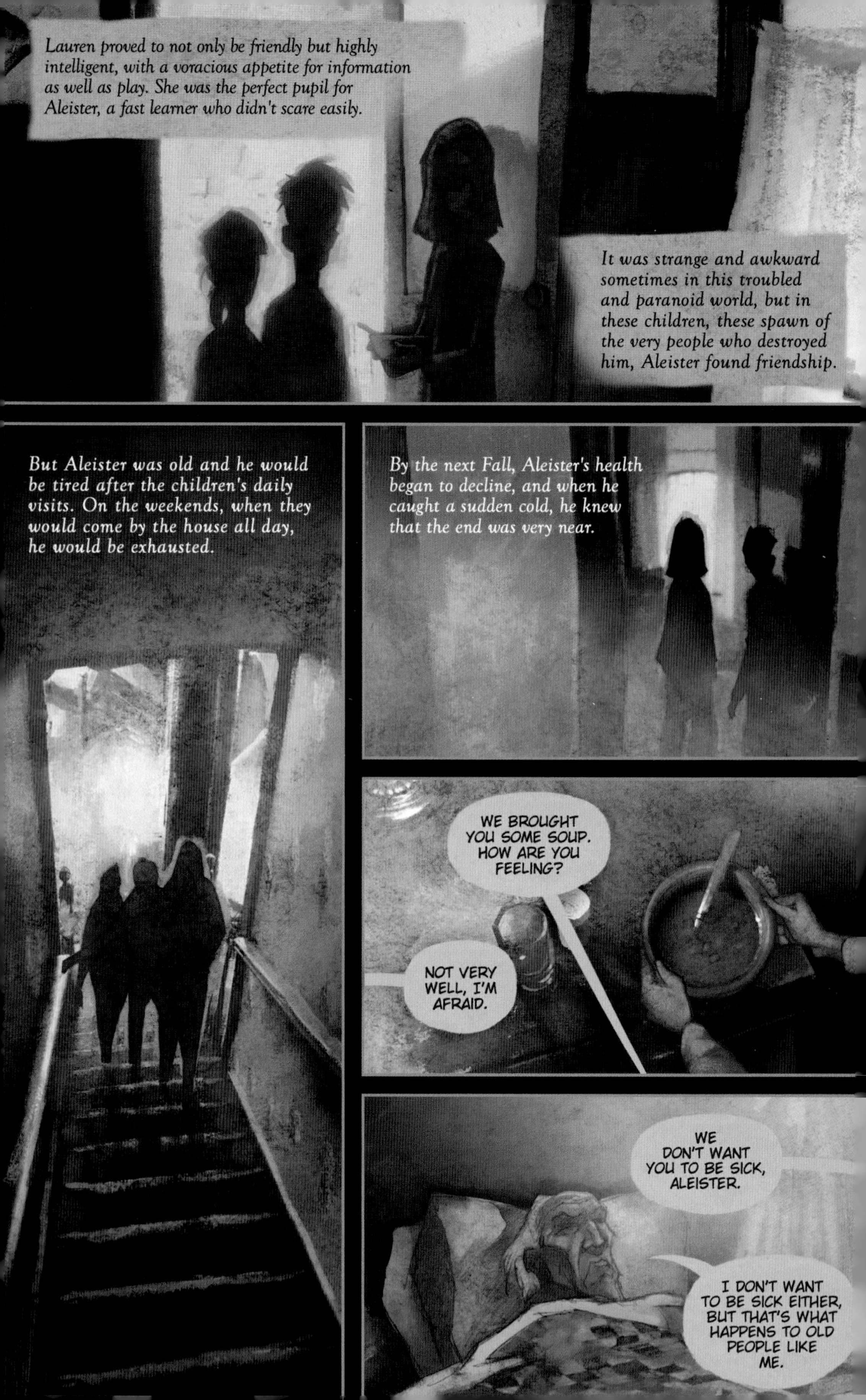
Lauren proved to not only be friendly but highly intelligent, with a voracious appetite for information as well as play. She was the perfect pupil for Aleister, a fast learner who didn't scare easily.
It was strange and awkward sometimes in this troubled and paranoid world, but in these children, these spawn of the very people who destroyed him, Aleister found friendship.
But Aleister was old and he would be tired after the children's daily visits. On the weekends, when they would come by the house all day, he would be exhausted.
By the next Fall, Aleister's health began to decline, and when he caught a sudden cold, he knew that the end was very near.
WE BROUGHT YOU SOME SOUP. HOW ARE YOU FEELING?
NOT VERY WELL, I'M AFRAID.
WE DON'T WANT YOU TO BE SICK, ALEISTER.
I DON'T WANT TO BE SICK EITHER, BUT THAT'S WHAT HAPPENS TO OLD PEOPLE LIKE ME.

BEFORE I GO... I HAVE TO TELL YOU SOMETHING.
WHAT'S THAT?
I WAS ANGRY FOR A LONG TIME AFTER YOUR PARENTS CAME AFTER ME AND MY SHOW. I WAS VERY ANGRY...
SO ANGRY.
ALEISTER?
P... PLEASE FORGIVE ME FOR WHAT I'VE DONE.
DONE? WHAT DO YOU MEAN?
SOMETHING TERRIBLE... EVERYTHING STARTS WITH ME... RUN... DEAD.
DARK SKIES... ONLY THE DEAD... RUN...
ALEISTER?

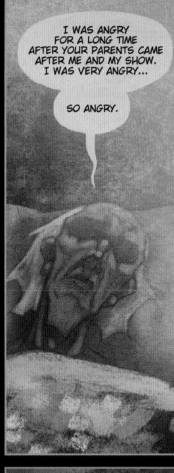

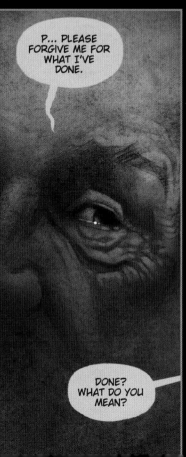

ALEISTER!
And with Aleister's death a fuse was lit, a trigger pulled, and Jackson, Oklahoma would pay dearly for its sins.

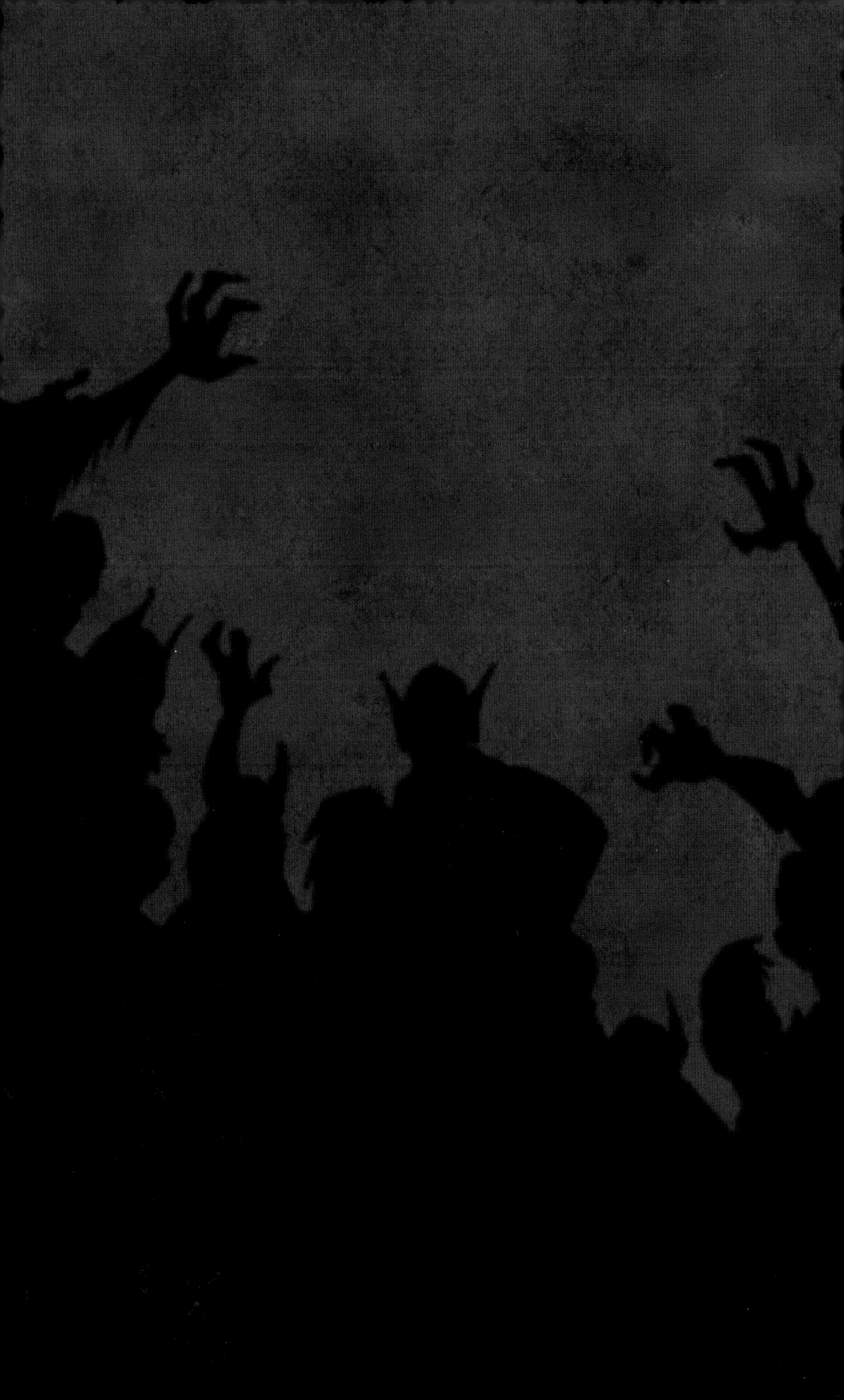

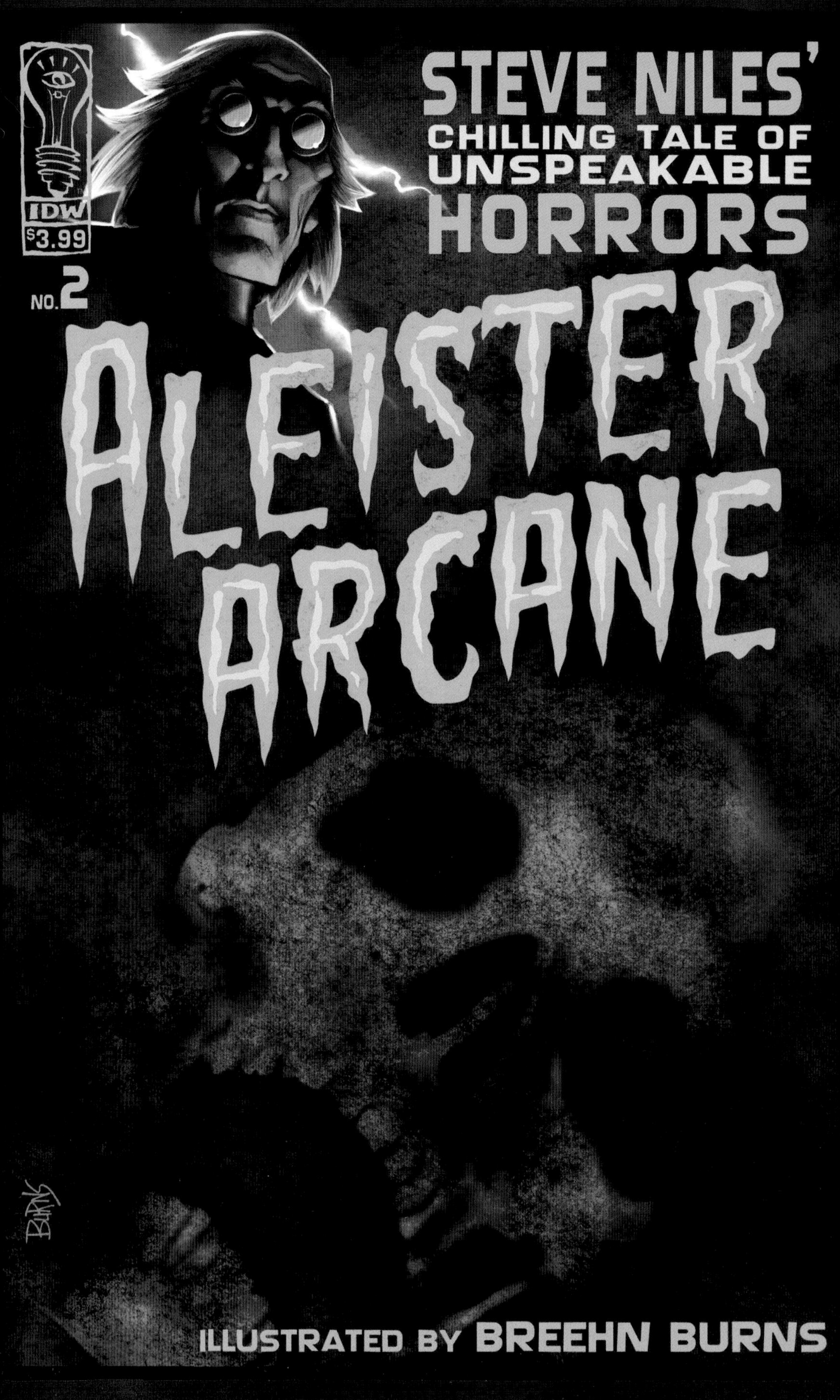
IDW
$3.99
NO. 2
STEVE NILES'
CHILLING TALE OF
UNSPEAKABLE
HORRORS
ALEISTER
ARCANE
BURNS
ILLUSTRATED BY BREEHN BURNS

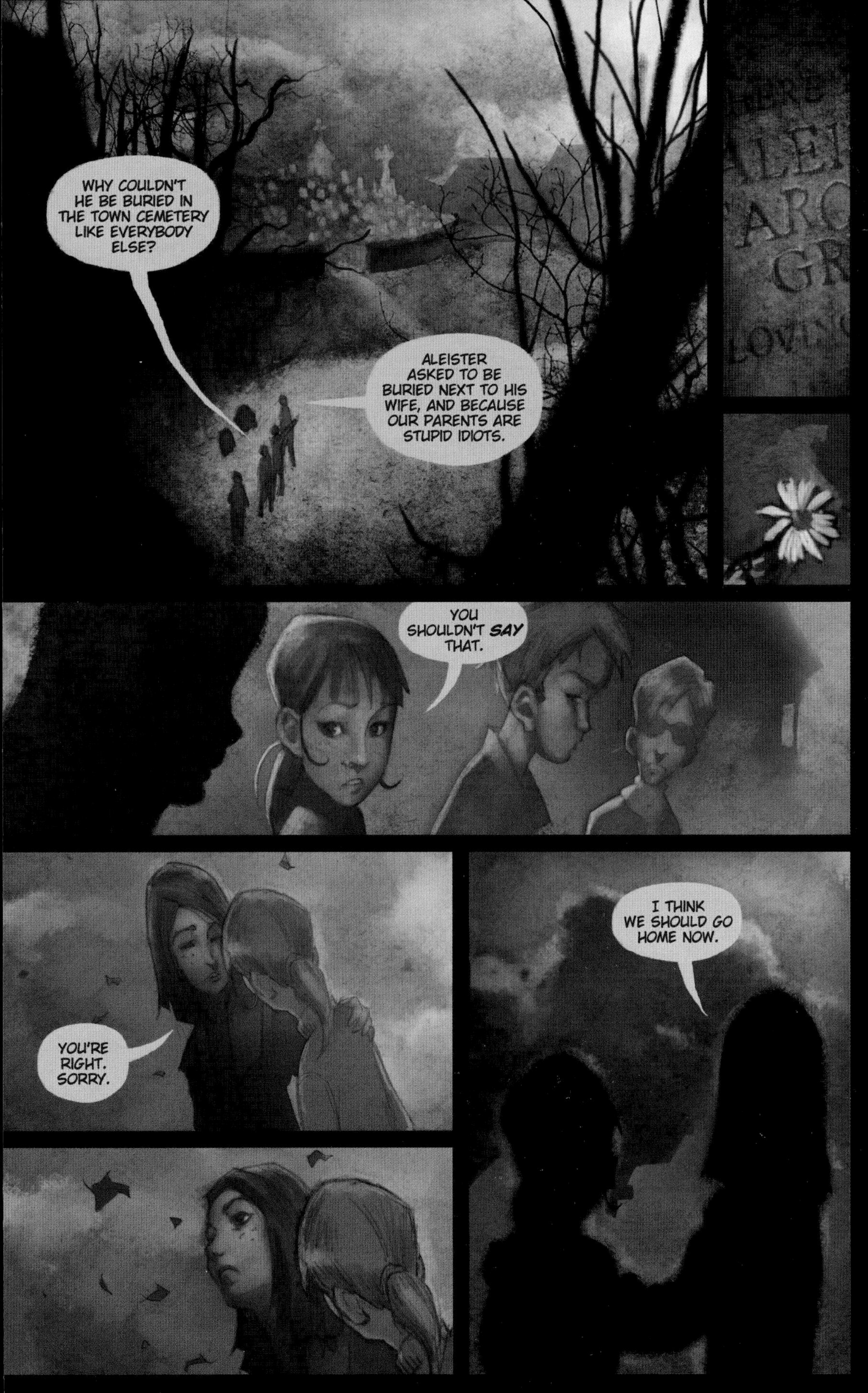
WHY COULDN'T HE BE BURIED IN THE TOWN CEMETERY LIKE EVERYBODY ELSE?
ALEISTER ASKED TO BE BURIED NEXT TO HIS WIFE, AND BECAUSE OUR PARENTS ARE STUPID IDIOTS.
YOU SHOULDN'T SAY THAT.
YOU'RE RIGHT. SORRY.
I THINK WE SHOULD GO HOME NOW.

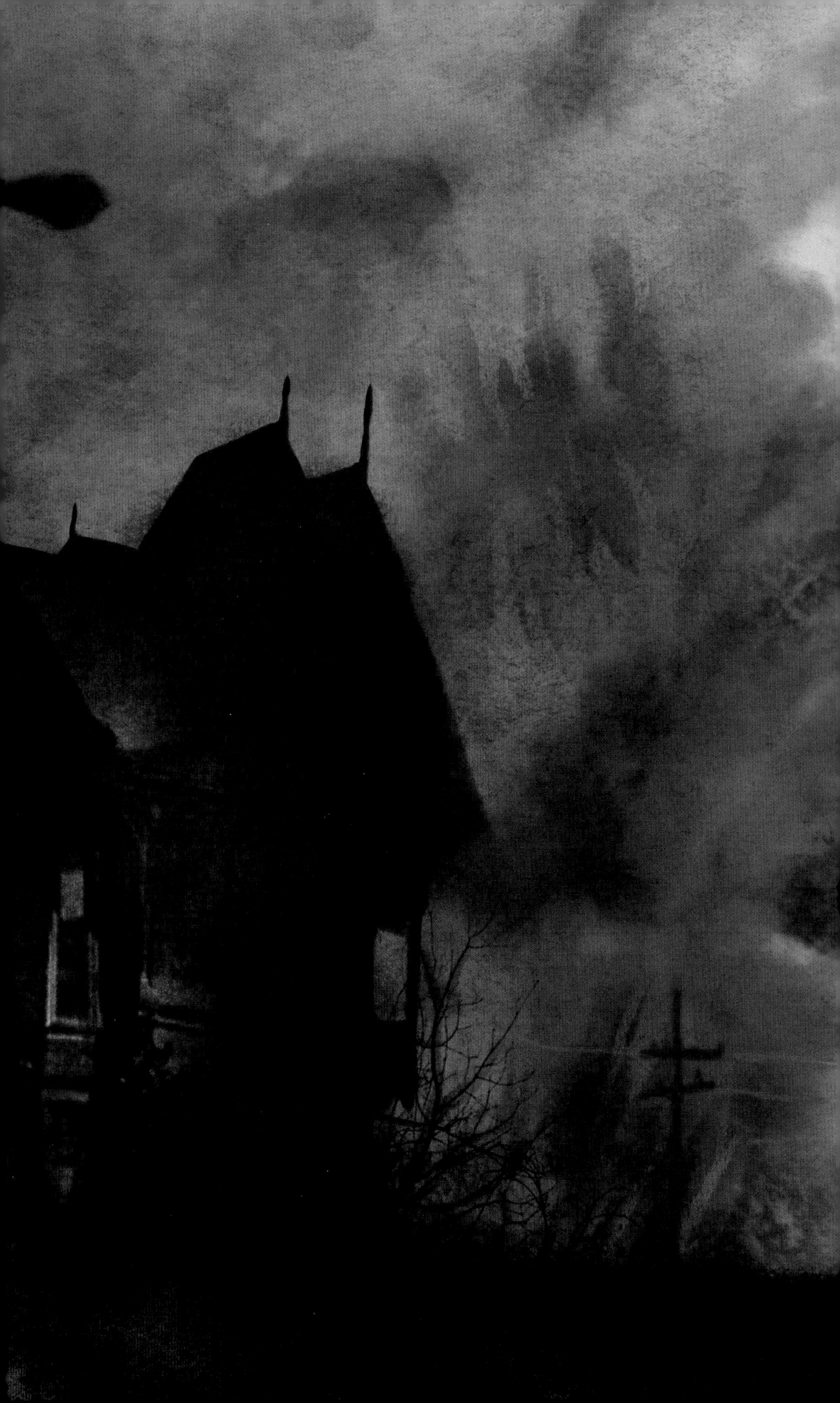

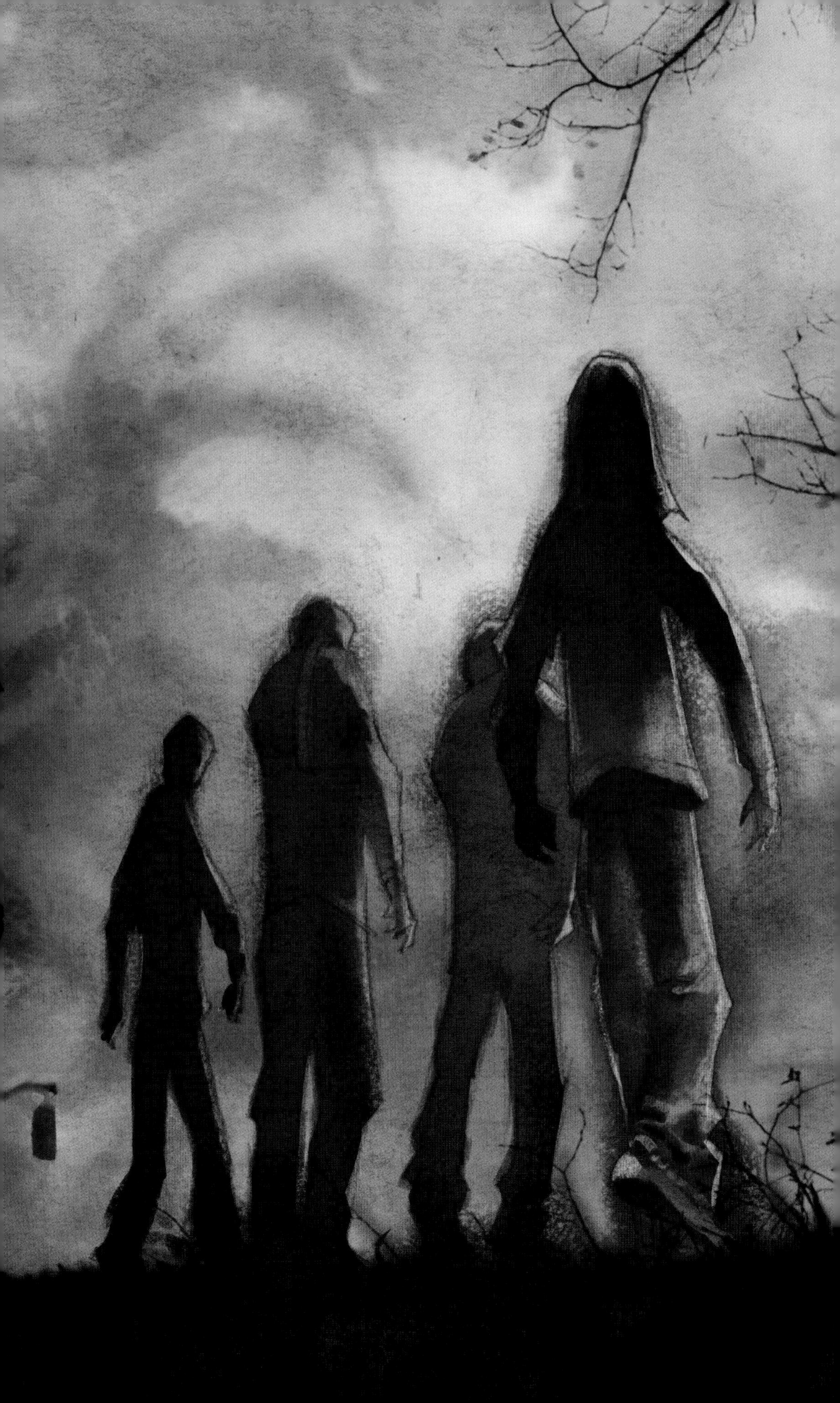

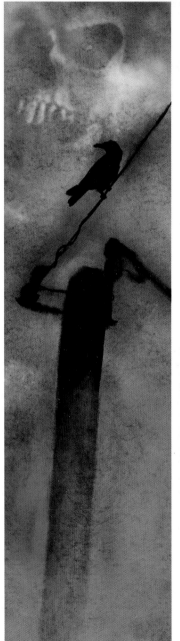

WHERE'S EVERYBODY AT?

THIS IS *CREEPY*.

I'LL WALK YOU ALL HOME.

MAYBE SOMETHING HAPPENED WHILE WE WERE AT ALEISTER'S GRAVE?

MAYBE.

SEE YOU GUYS TOMORROW.

SEE YA, JACOB.

B... BYE.

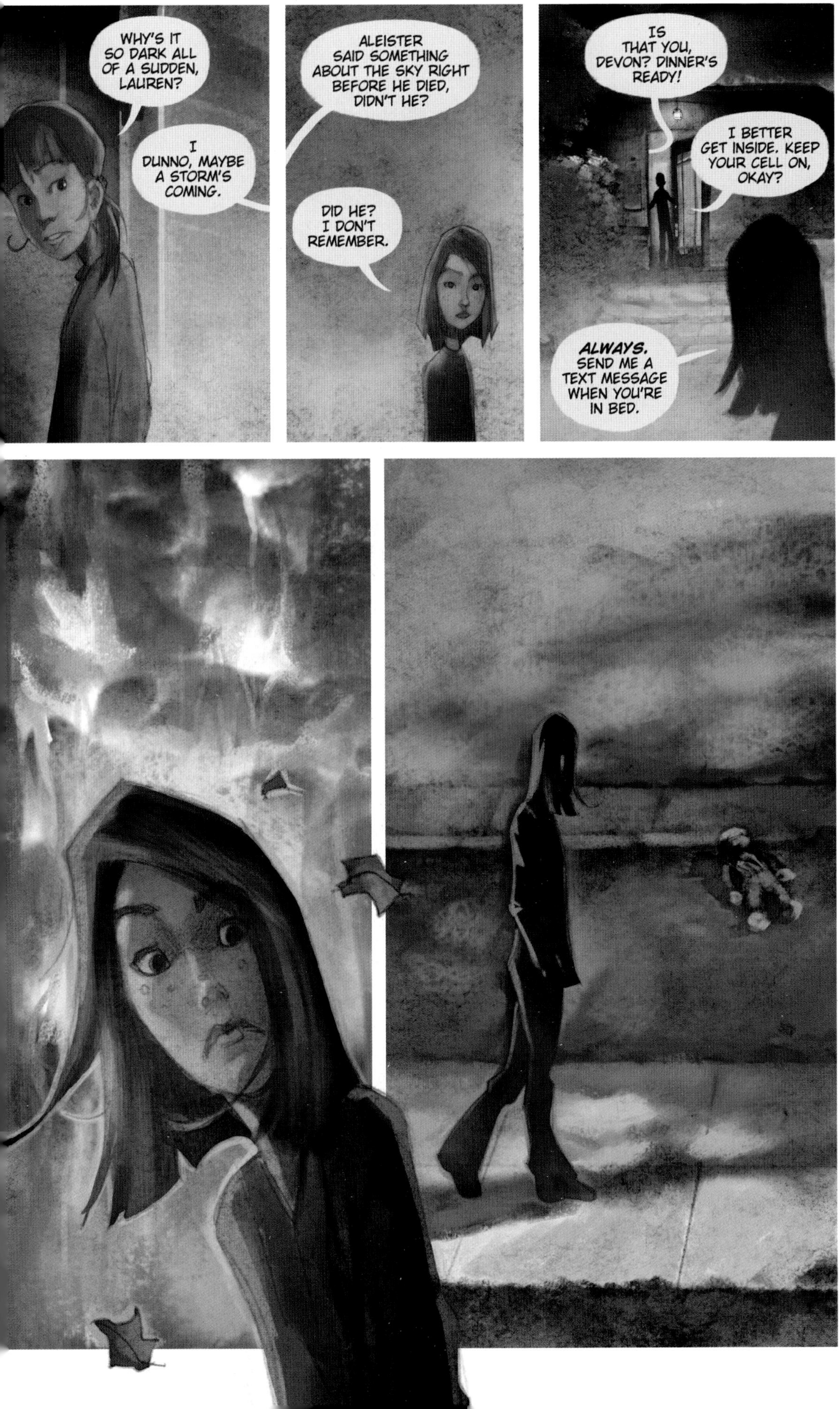
WHY'S IT SO DARK ALL OF A SUDDEN, LAUREN?
I DUNNO, MAYBE A STORM'S COMING.
ALEISTER SAID SOMETHING ABOUT THE SKY RIGHT BEFORE HE DIED, DIDN'T HE?
DID HE? I DON'T REMEMBER.
IS THAT YOU, DEVON? DINNER'S READY!
I BETTER GET INSIDE. KEEP YOUR CELL ON, OKAY?
ALWAYS. SEND ME A TEXT MESSAGE WHEN YOU'RE IN BED.

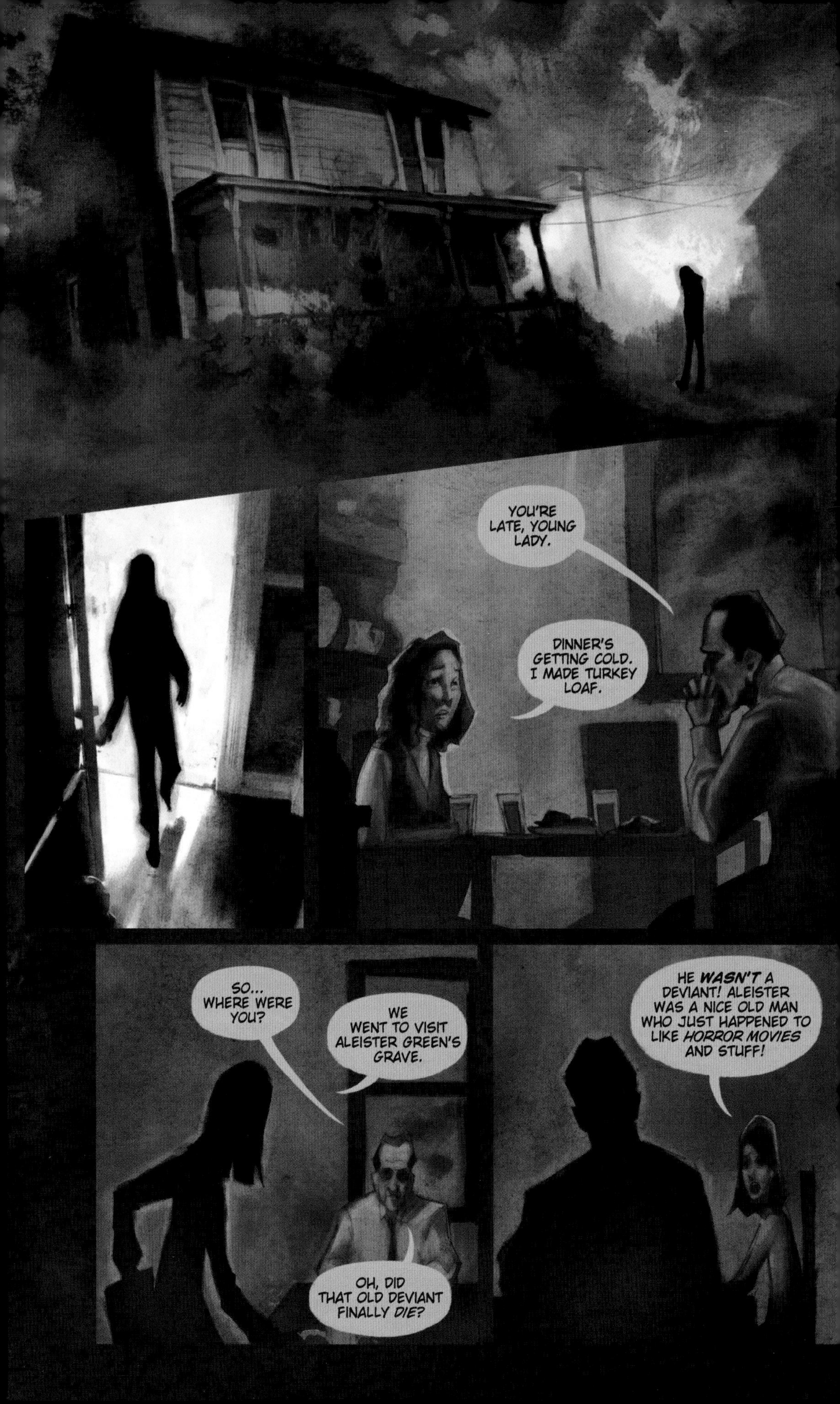
YOU'RE LATE, YOUNG LADY.
DINNER'S GETTING COLD. I MADE TURKEY LOAF.
SO... WHERE WERE YOU?
WE WENT TO VISIT ALEISTER GREEN'S GRAVE.
OH, DID THAT OLD DEVIANT FINALLY *DIE*?
HE ***WASN'T*** A DEVIANT! ALEISTER WAS A NICE OLD MAN WHO JUST HAPPENED TO LIKE *HORROR MOVIES* AND STUFF!

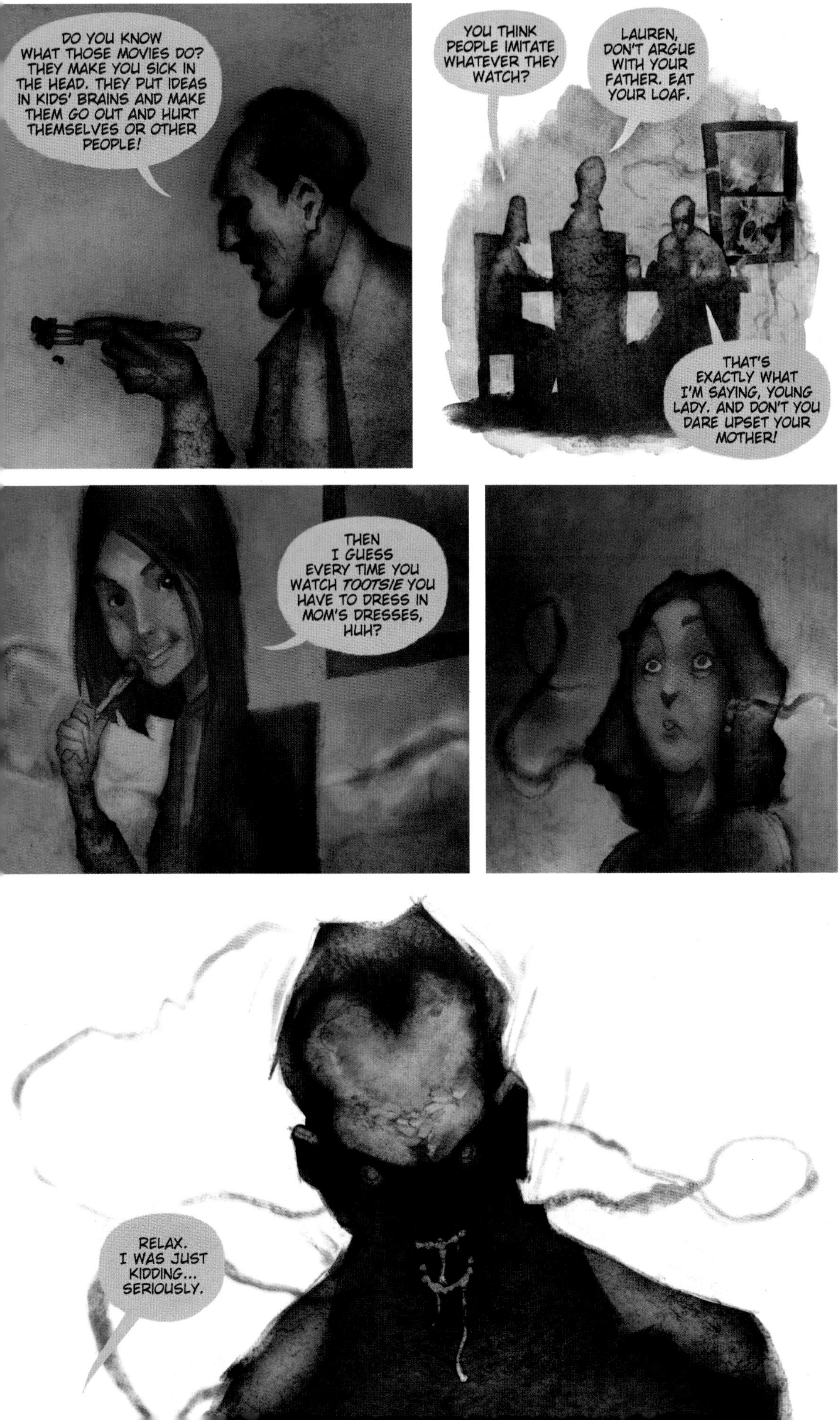
DO YOU KNOW WHAT THOSE MOVIES DO? THEY MAKE YOU SICK IN THE HEAD. THEY PUT IDEAS IN KIDS' BRAINS AND MAKE THEM GO OUT AND HURT THEMSELVES OR OTHER PEOPLE!
YOU THINK PEOPLE IMITATE WHATEVER THEY WATCH?
LAUREN, DON'T ARGUE WITH YOUR FATHER. EAT YOUR LOAF.
THAT'S EXACTLY WHAT I'M SAYING, YOUNG LADY. AND DON'T YOU DARE UPSET YOUR MOTHER!
THEN I GUESS EVERY TIME YOU WATCH *TOOTSIE* YOU HAVE TO DRESS IN MOM'S DRESSES, HUH?
RELAX. I WAS JUST KIDDING... SERIOUSLY.

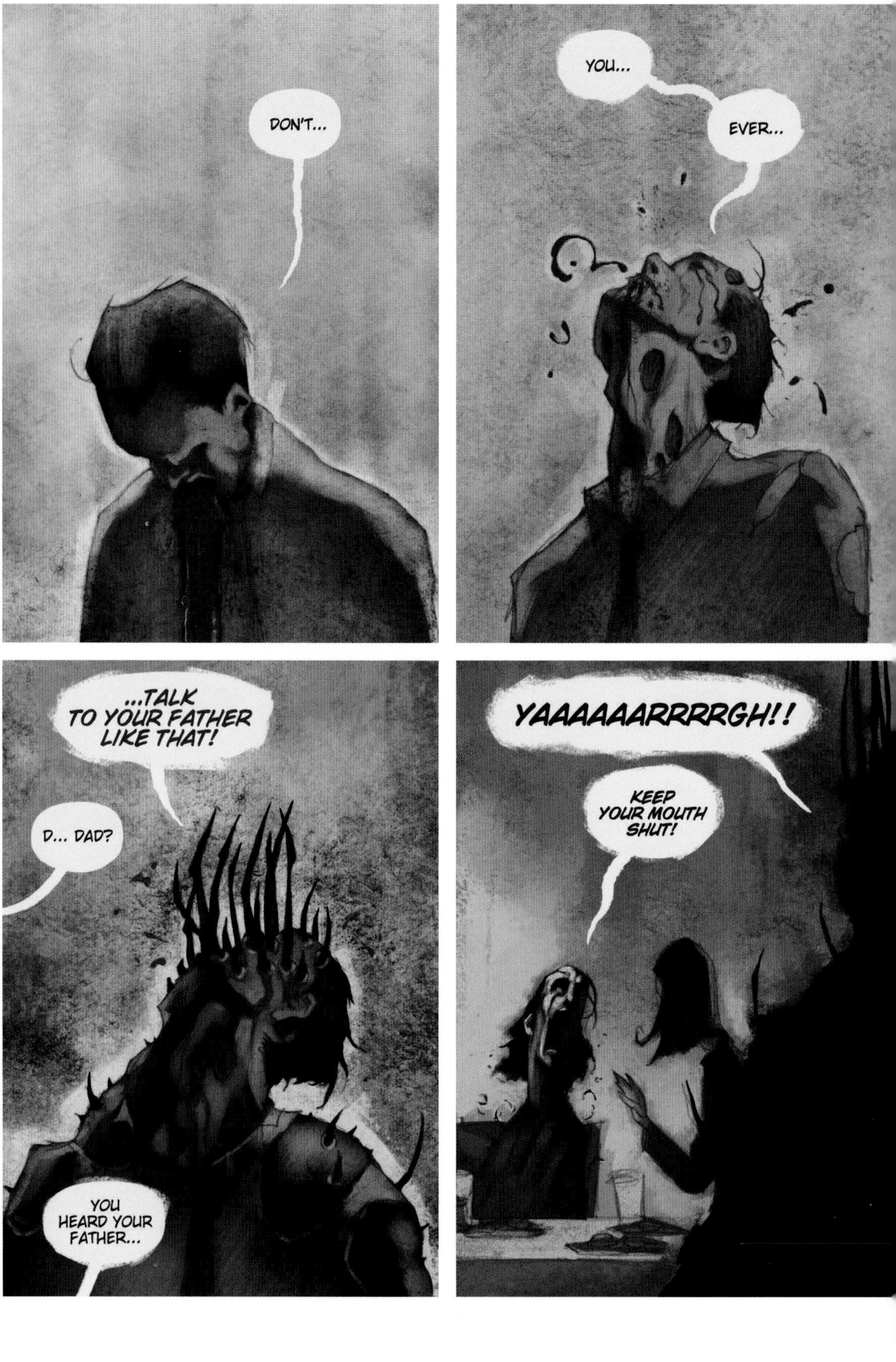
DON'T...
YOU...
EVER...
...TALK TO YOUR FATHER LIKE THAT!
D... DAD?
YOU HEARD YOUR FATHER...
YAAAAAARRRRGH!!
KEEP YOUR MOUTH SHUT!

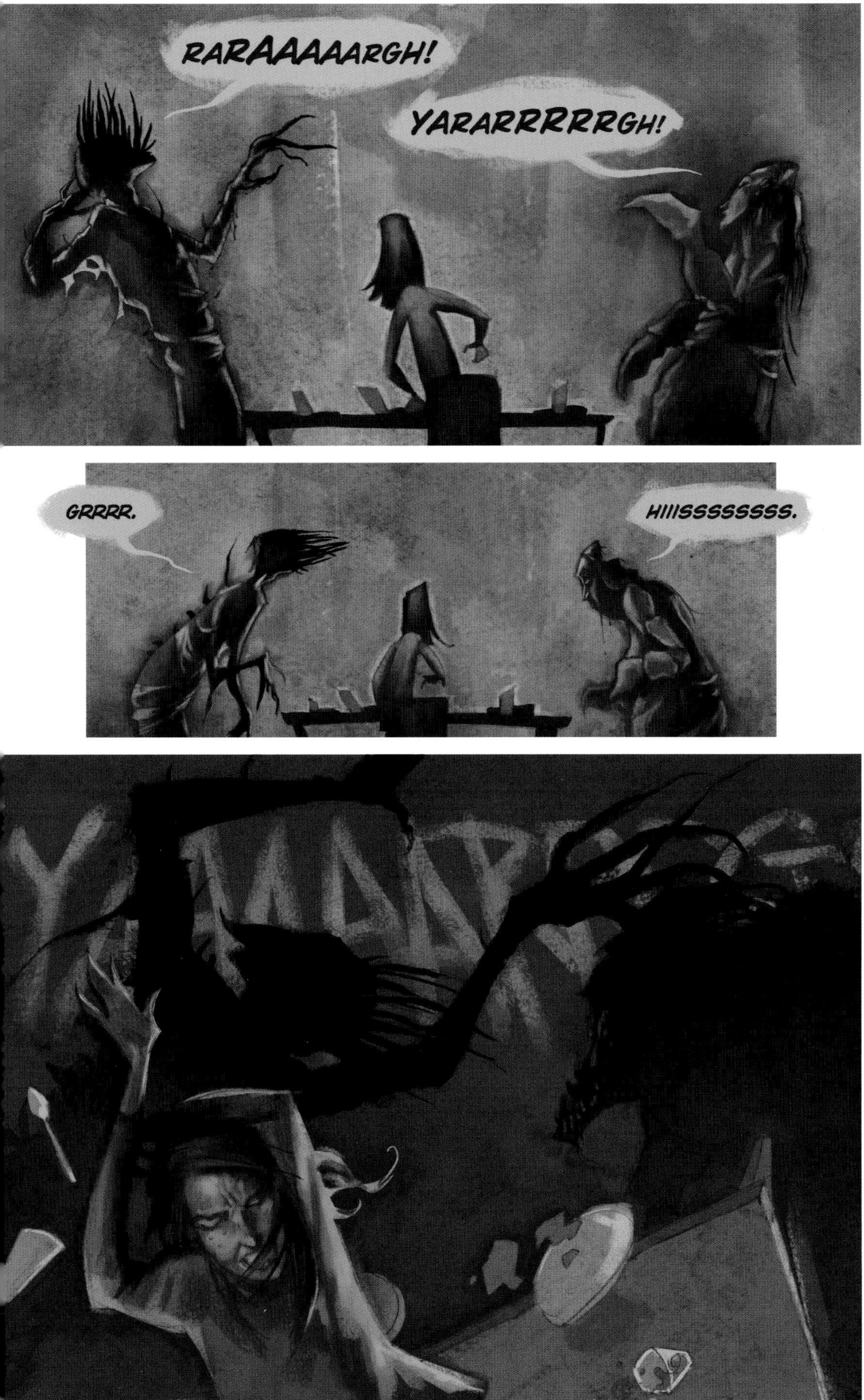
RARAAAAAARGH!
YARARRRRRRGH!
GRRRR.
HIIISSSSSSSS.

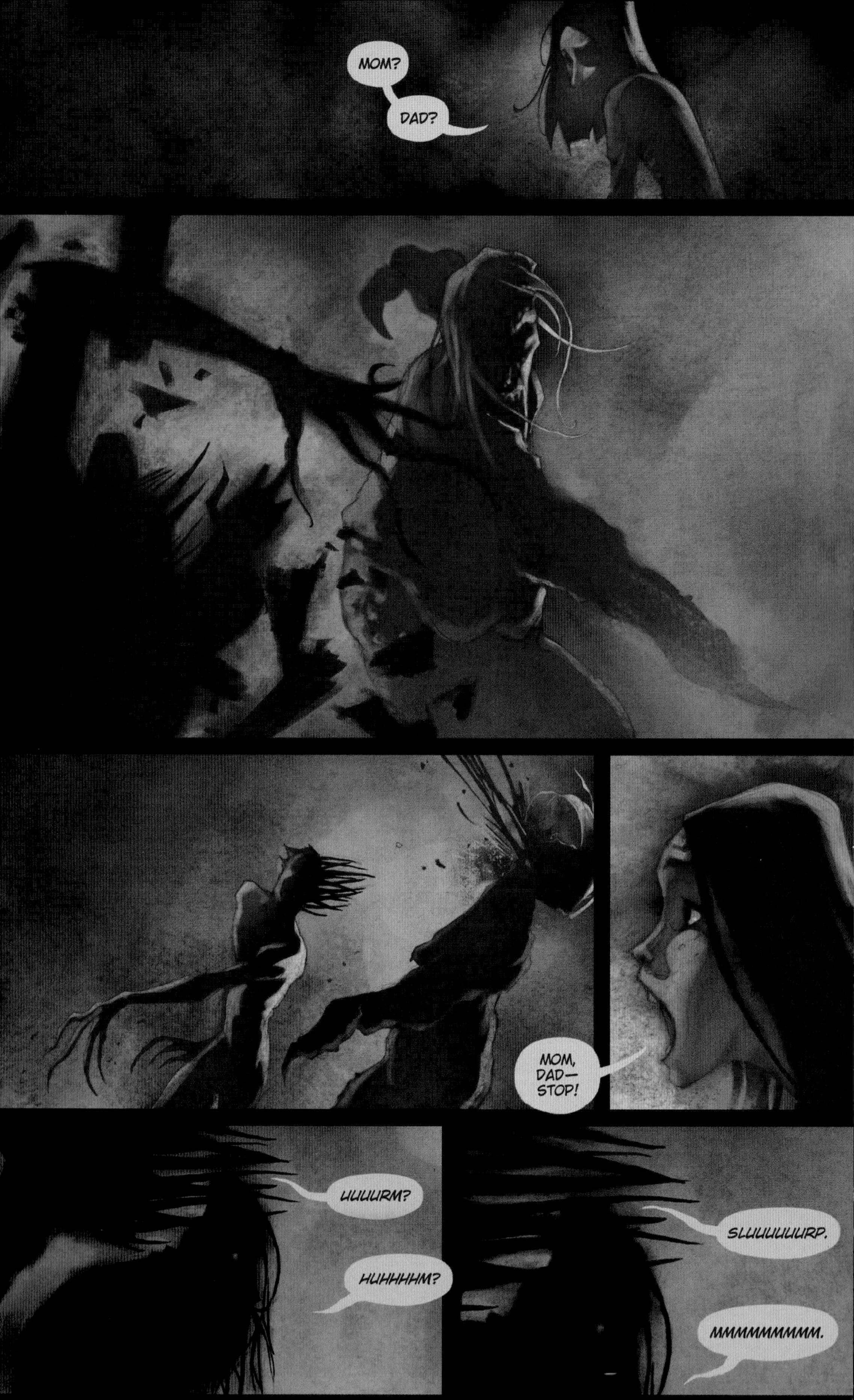
MOM?
DAD?
MOM, DAD— STOP!
UUUURM?
HUHHHHM?
SLUUUUUURP.
MMMMMMMMM.

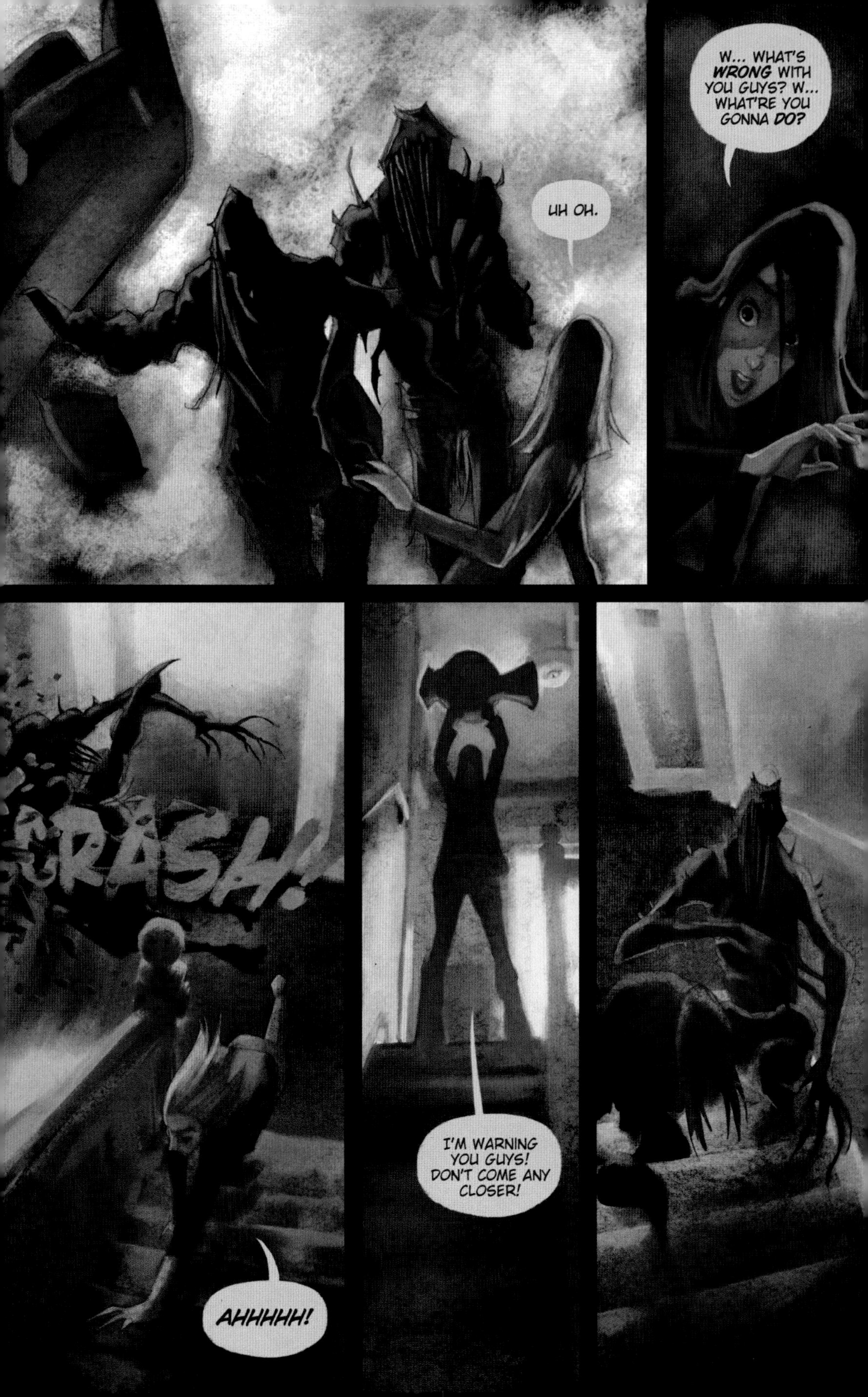
UH OH.
W... WHAT'S **WRONG** WITH YOU GUYS? W... WHAT'RE YOU GONNA **DO?**
CRASH!!
AHHHHH!
I'M WARNING YOU GUYS! DON'T COME ANY CLOSER!

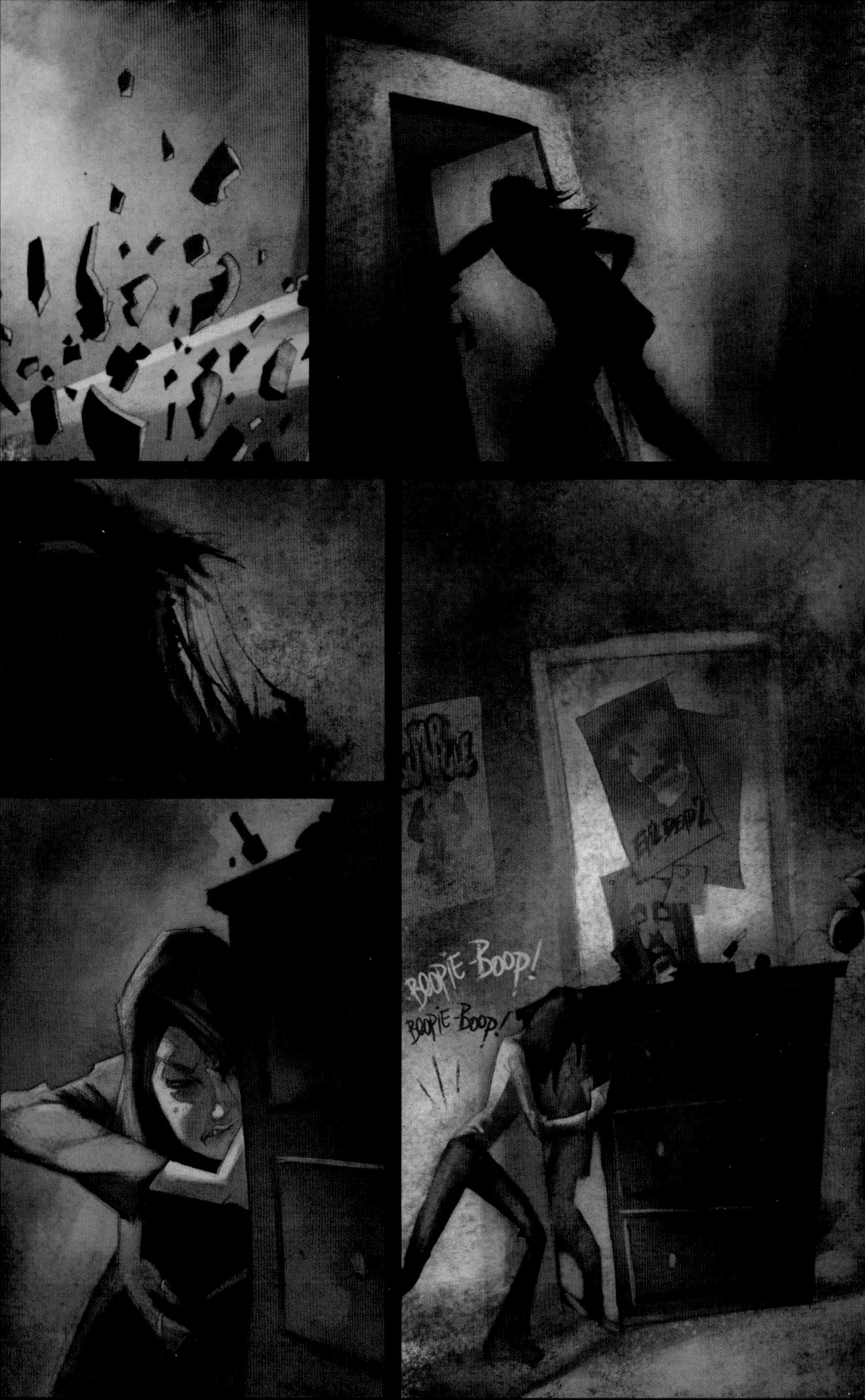
EVIL DEAD 2
BOOPIE-BOOP!
BOOPIE-BOOP!

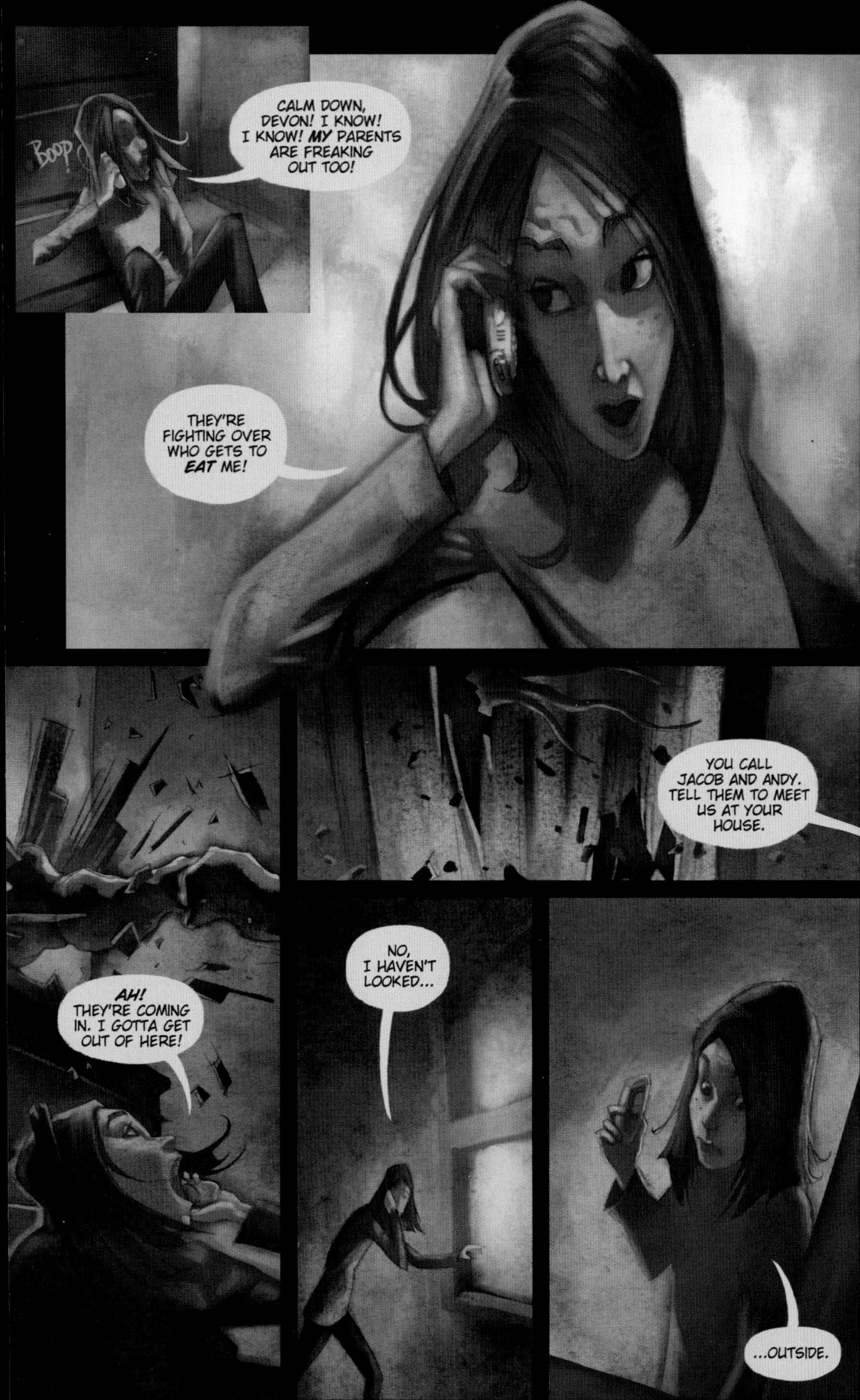
BOOP!
CALM DOWN, DEVON! I KNOW! I KNOW! MY PARENTS ARE FREAKING OUT TOO!
THEY'RE FIGHTING OVER WHO GETS TO EAT ME!
YOU CALL JACOB AND ANDY. TELL THEM TO MEET US AT YOUR HOUSE.
AH! THEY'RE COMING IN. I GOTTA GET OUT OF HERE!
NO, I HAVEN'T LOOKED...
...OUTSIDE.

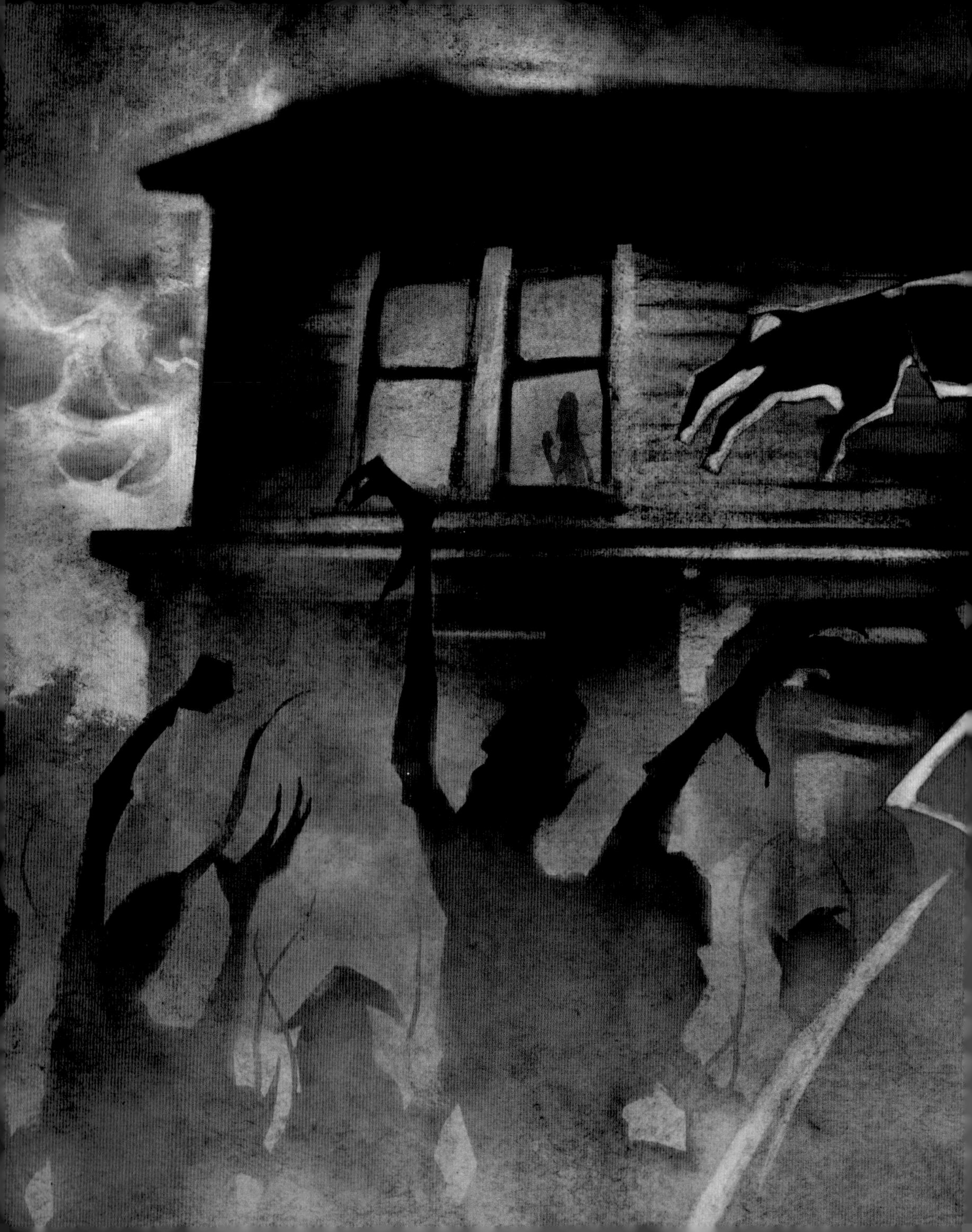

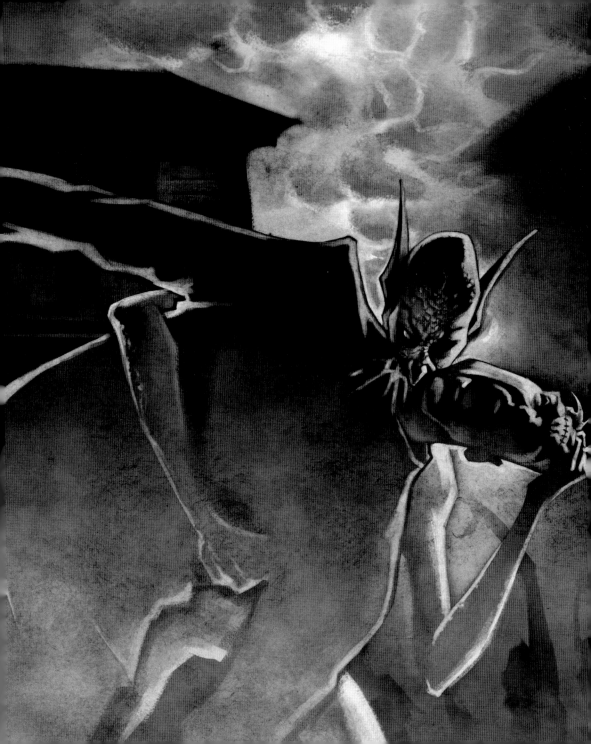

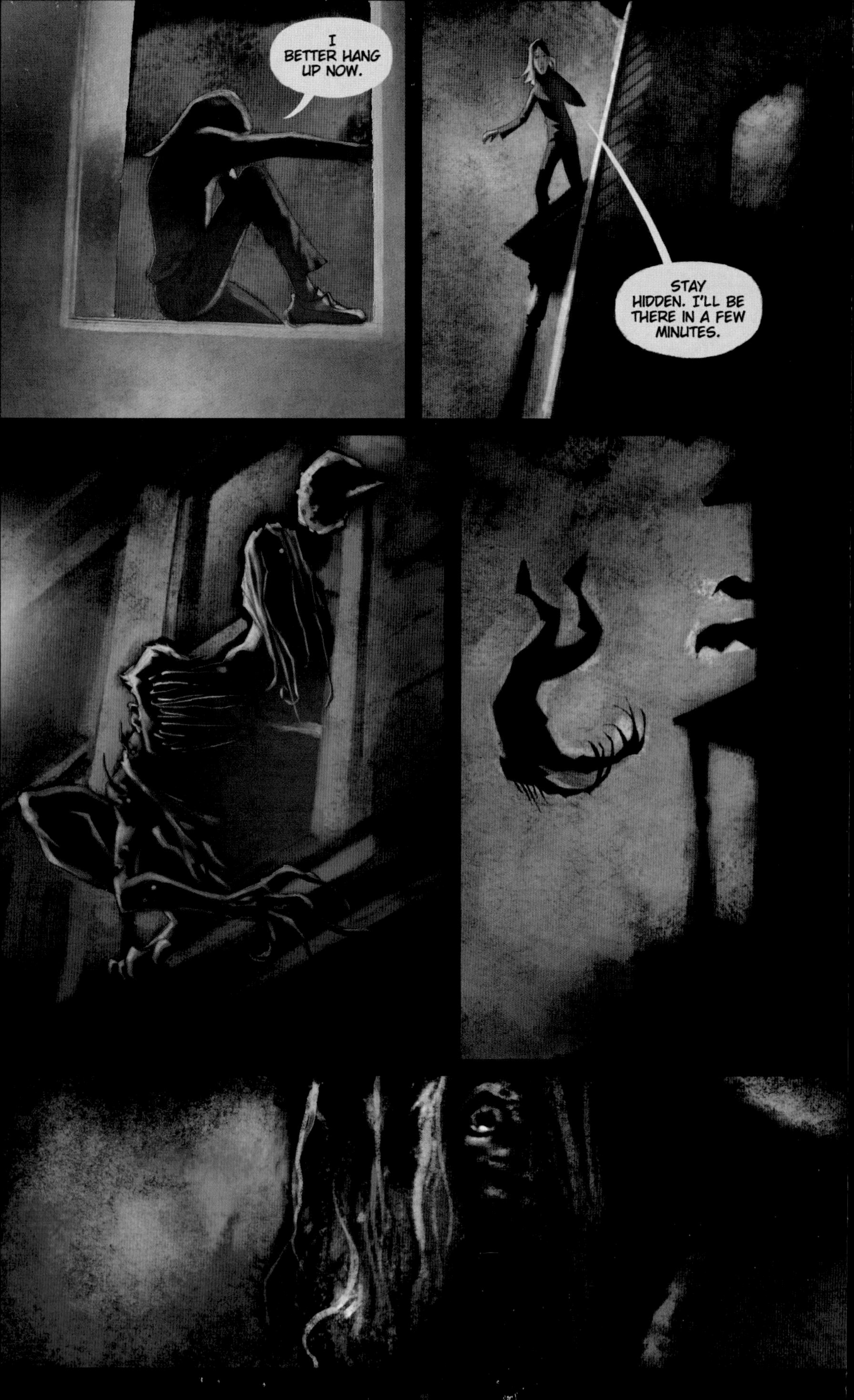
I BETTER HANG UP NOW.
STAY HIDDEN. I'LL BE THERE IN A FEW MINUTES.

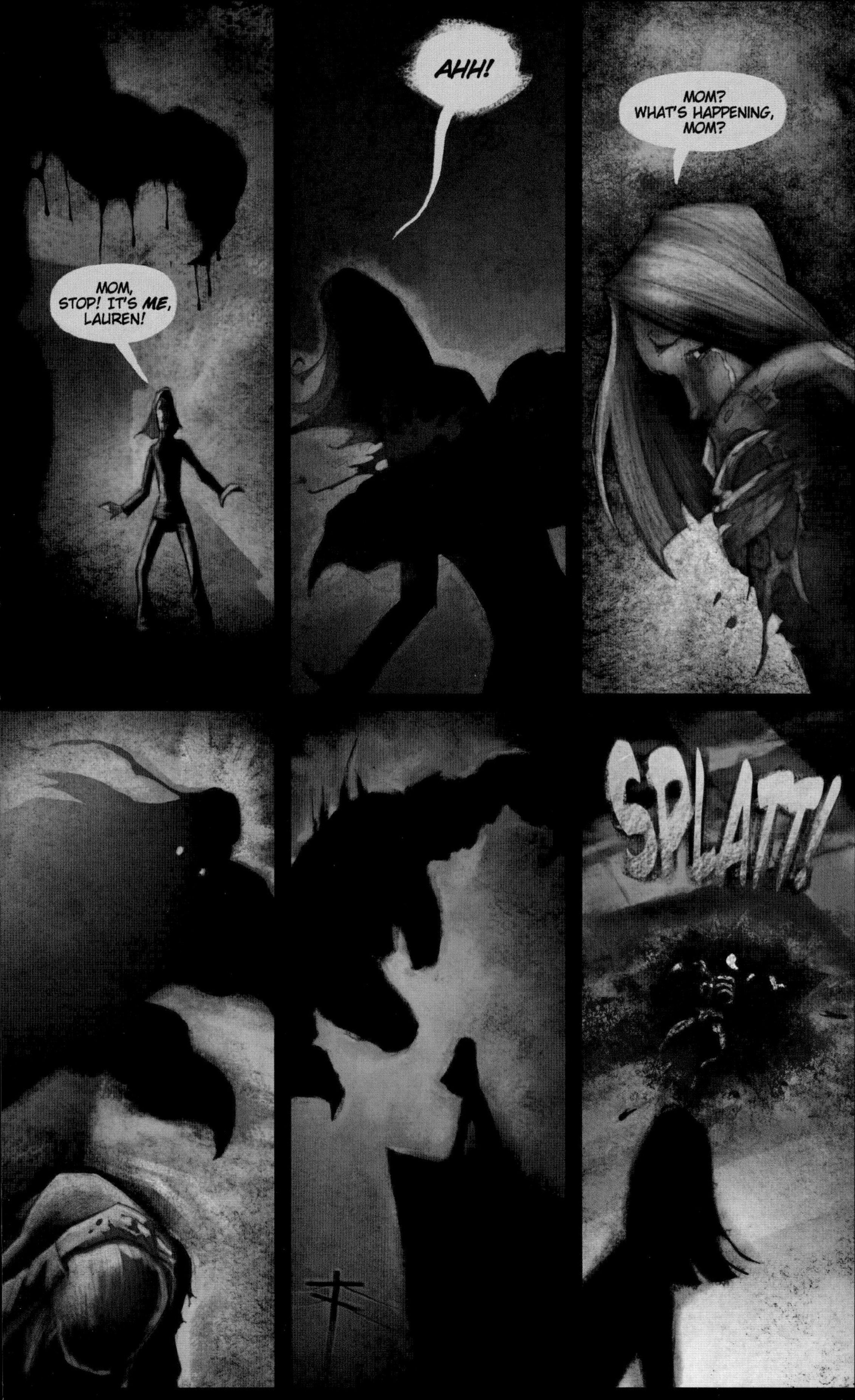
MOM, STOP! IT'S *ME*, LAUREN!
AHH!
MOM? WHAT'S HAPPENING, MOM?
SPLATT!

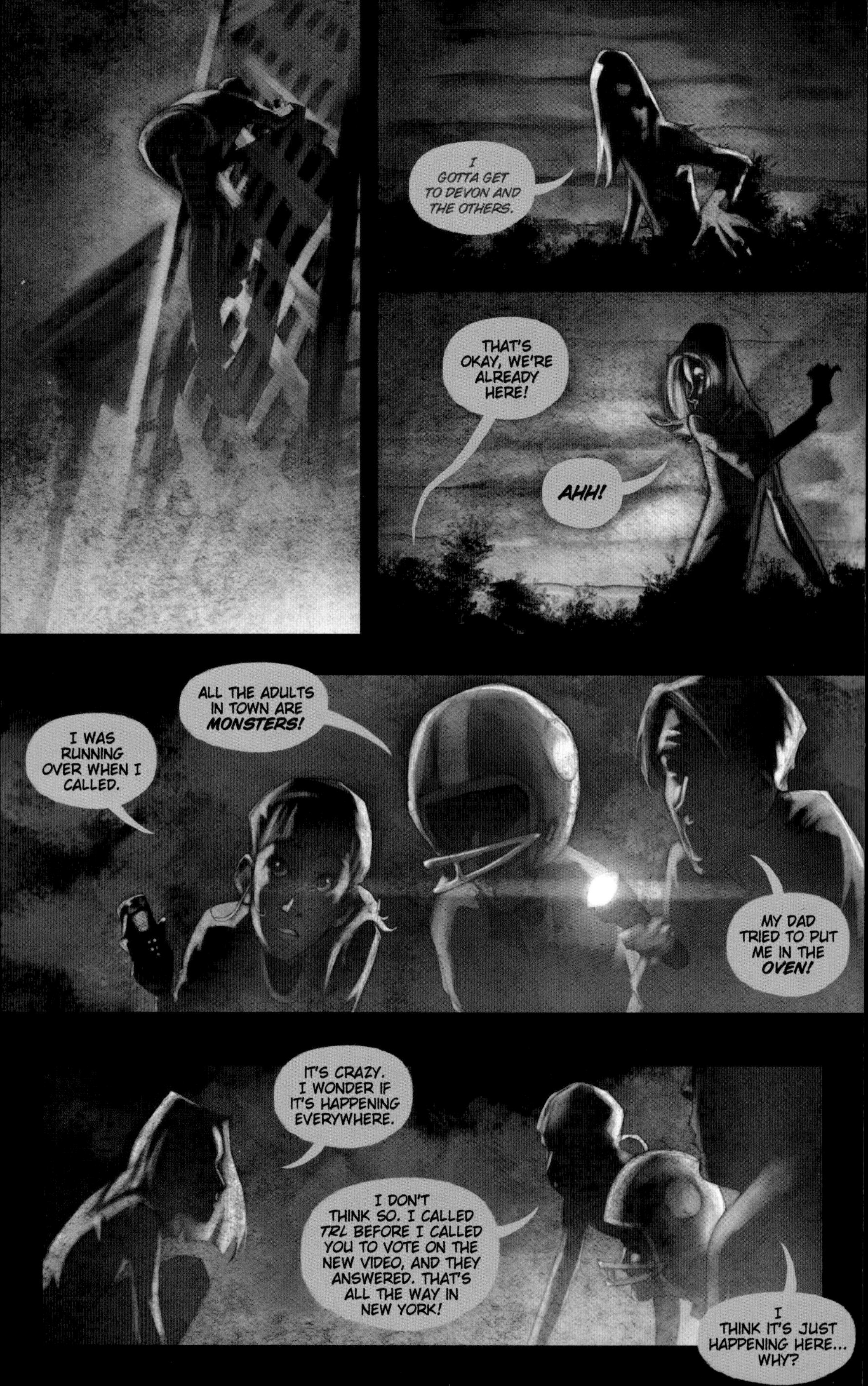
I GOTTA GET TO DEVON AND THE OTHERS.
THAT'S OKAY, WE'RE ALREADY HERE!
AHH!
I WAS RUNNING OVER WHEN I CALLED.
ALL THE ADULTS IN TOWN ARE MONSTERS!
MY DAD TRIED TO PUT ME IN THE OVEN!
IT'S CRAZY. I WONDER IF IT'S HAPPENING EVERYWHERE.
I DON'T THINK SO. I CALLED TRL BEFORE I CALLED YOU TO VOTE ON THE NEW VIDEO, AND THEY ANSWERED. THAT'S ALL THE WAY IN NEW YORK!
I THINK IT'S JUST HAPPENING HERE... WHY?

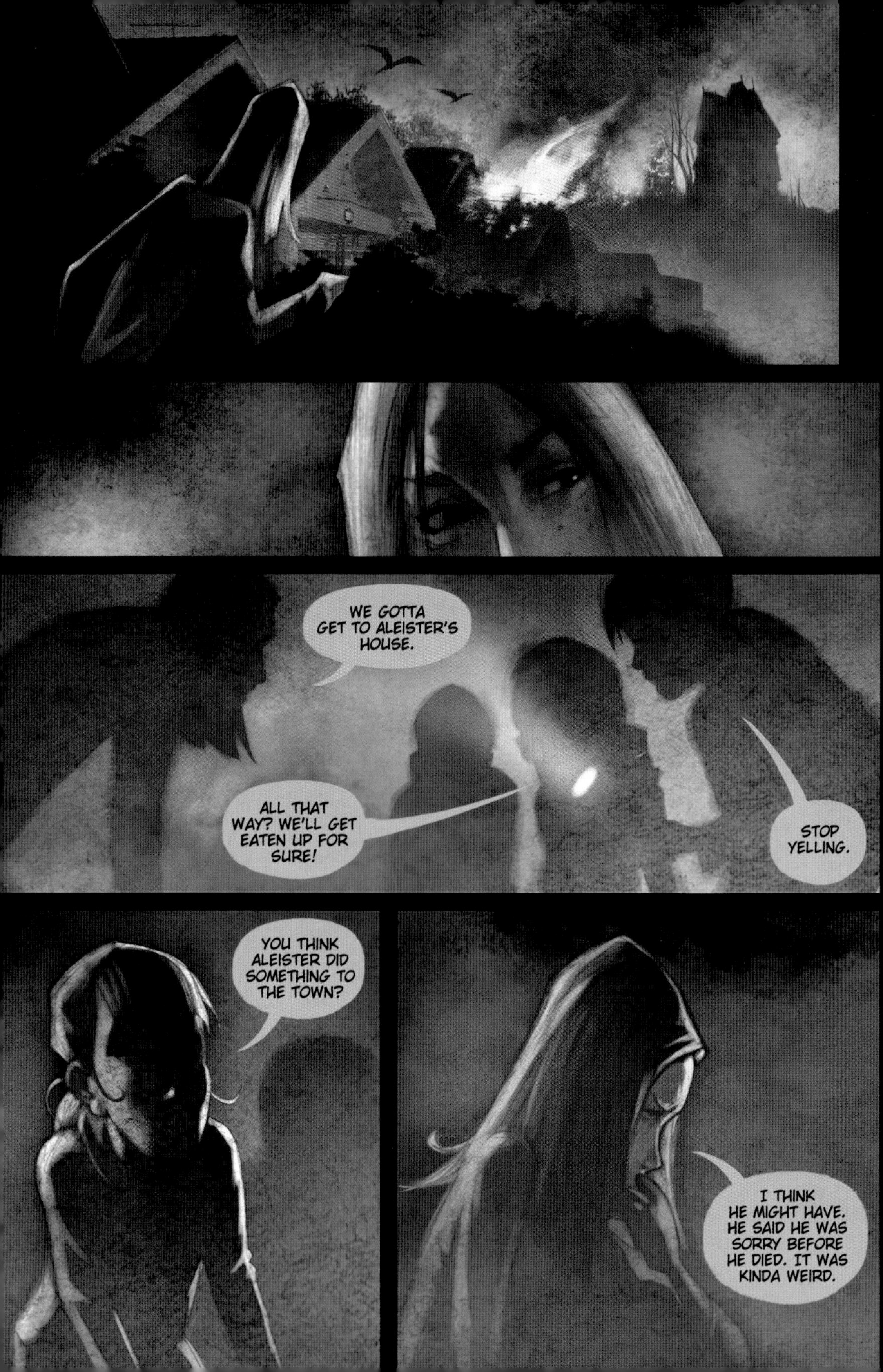
WE GOTTA GET TO ALEISTER'S HOUSE.
ALL THAT WAY? WE'LL GET EATEN UP FOR SURE!
STOP YELLING.
YOU THINK ALEISTER DID SOMETHING TO THE TOWN?
I THINK HE MIGHT HAVE. HE SAID HE WAS SORRY BEFORE HE DIED. IT WAS KINDA WEIRD.

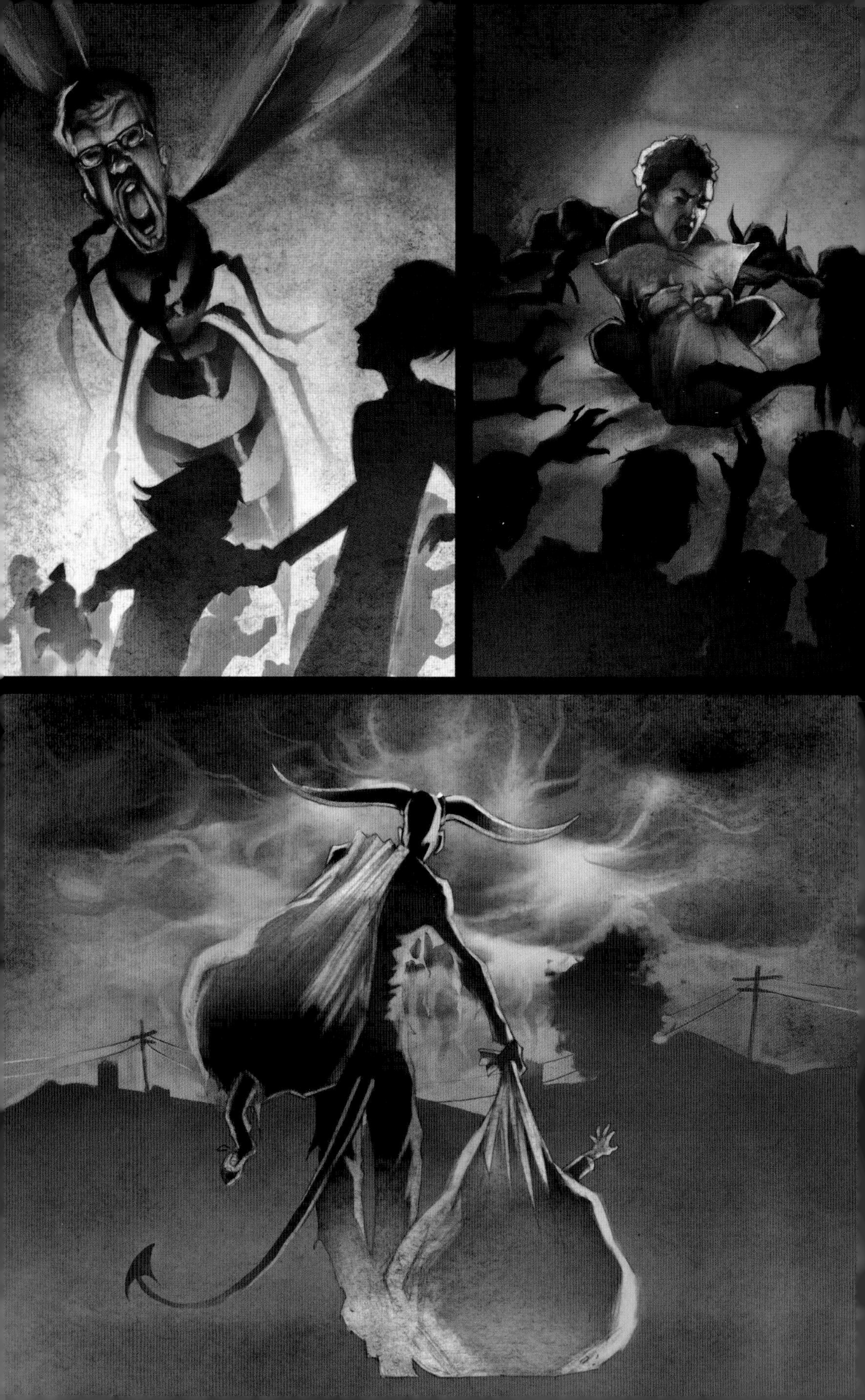

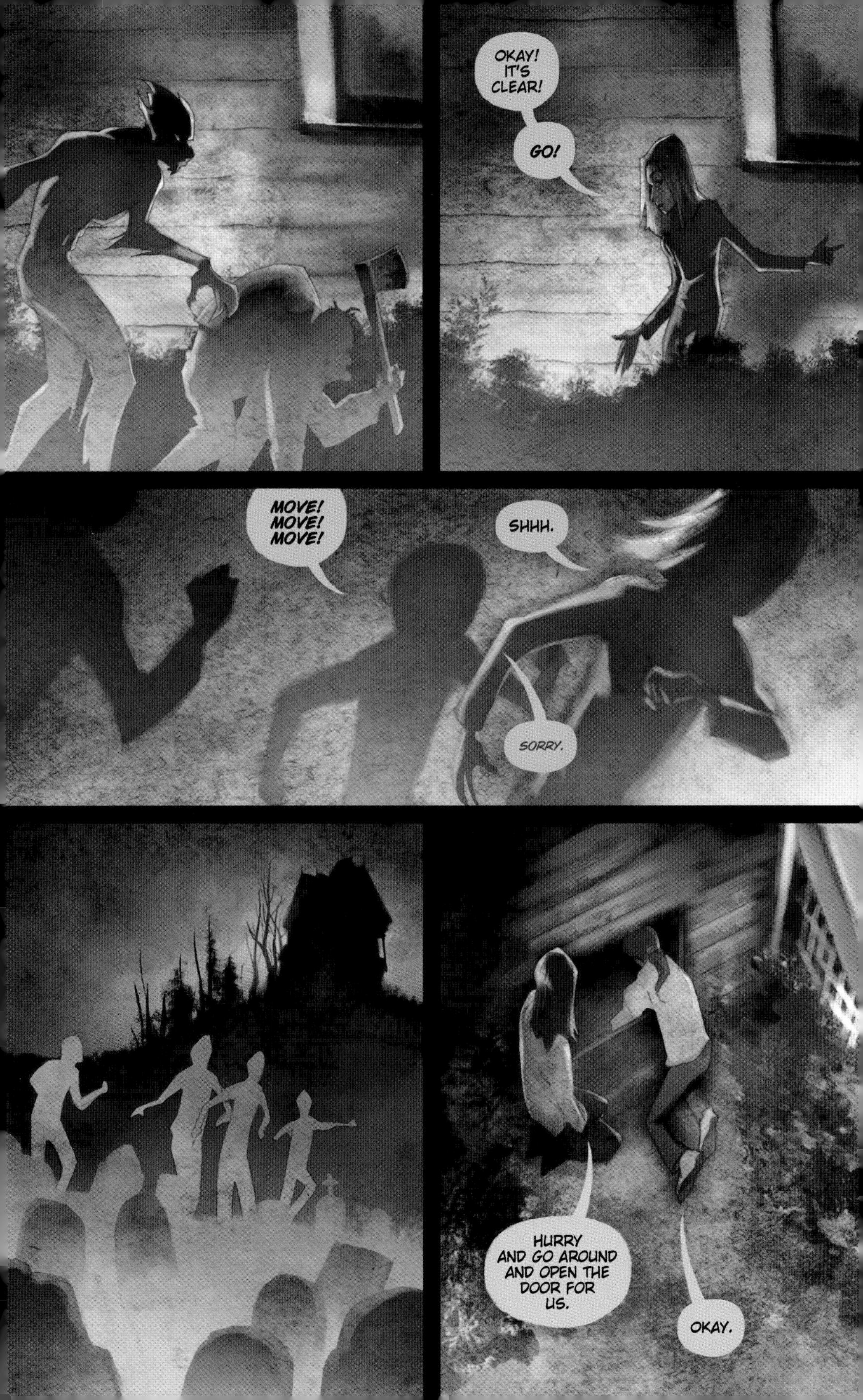
OKAY! IT'S CLEAR!
GO!
MOVE! MOVE! MOVE!
SHHH.
SORRY.
HURRY AND GO AROUND AND OPEN THE DOOR FOR US.
OKAY.

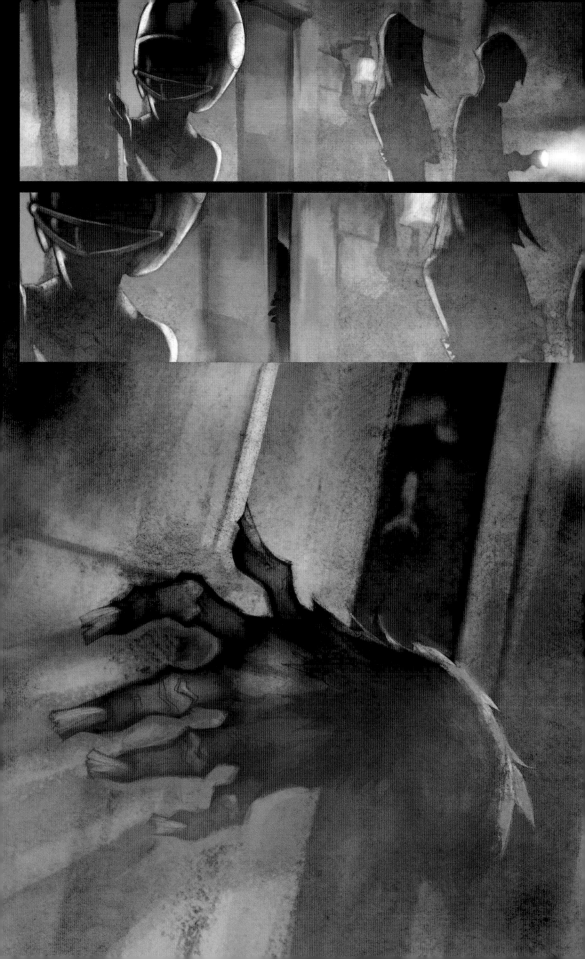

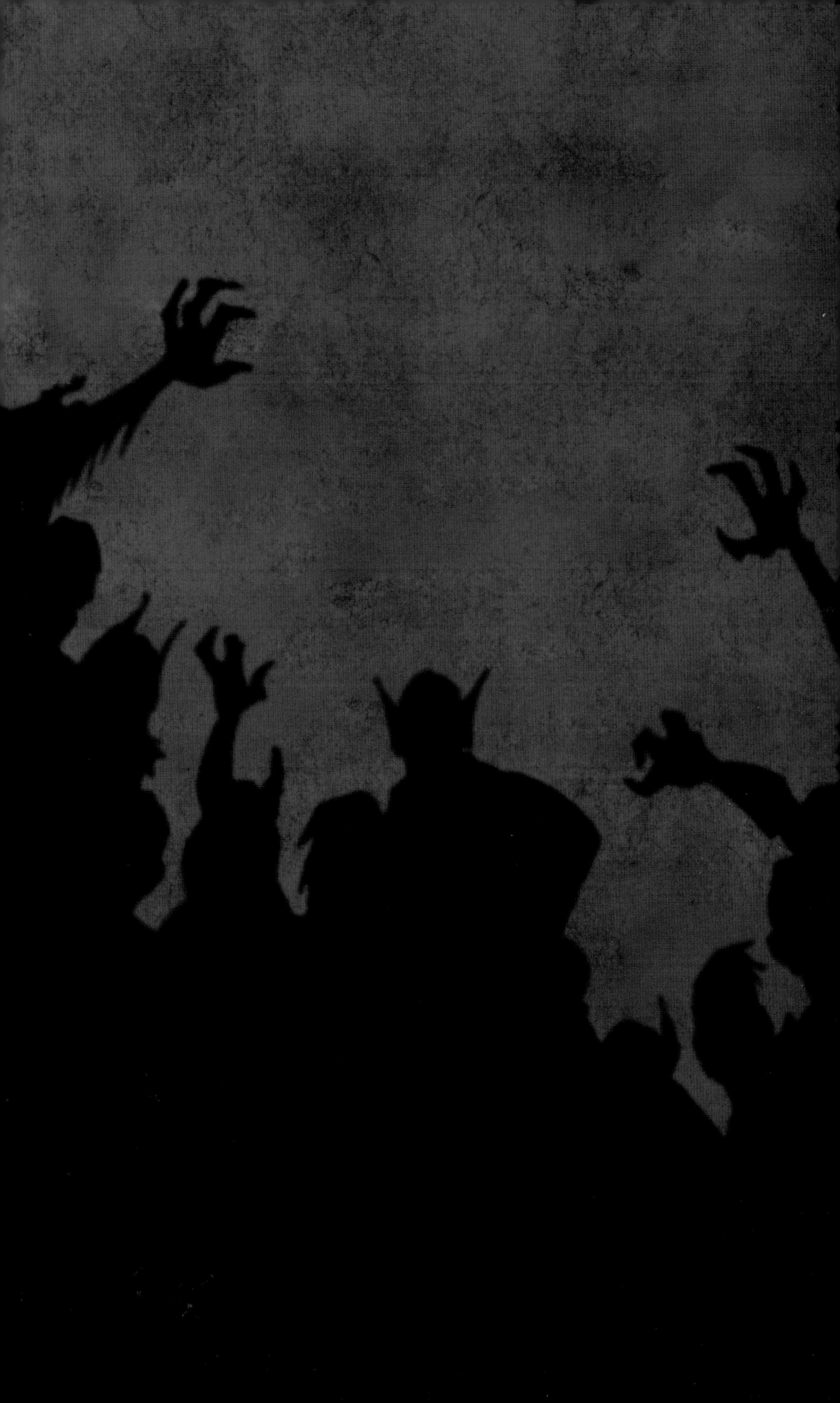

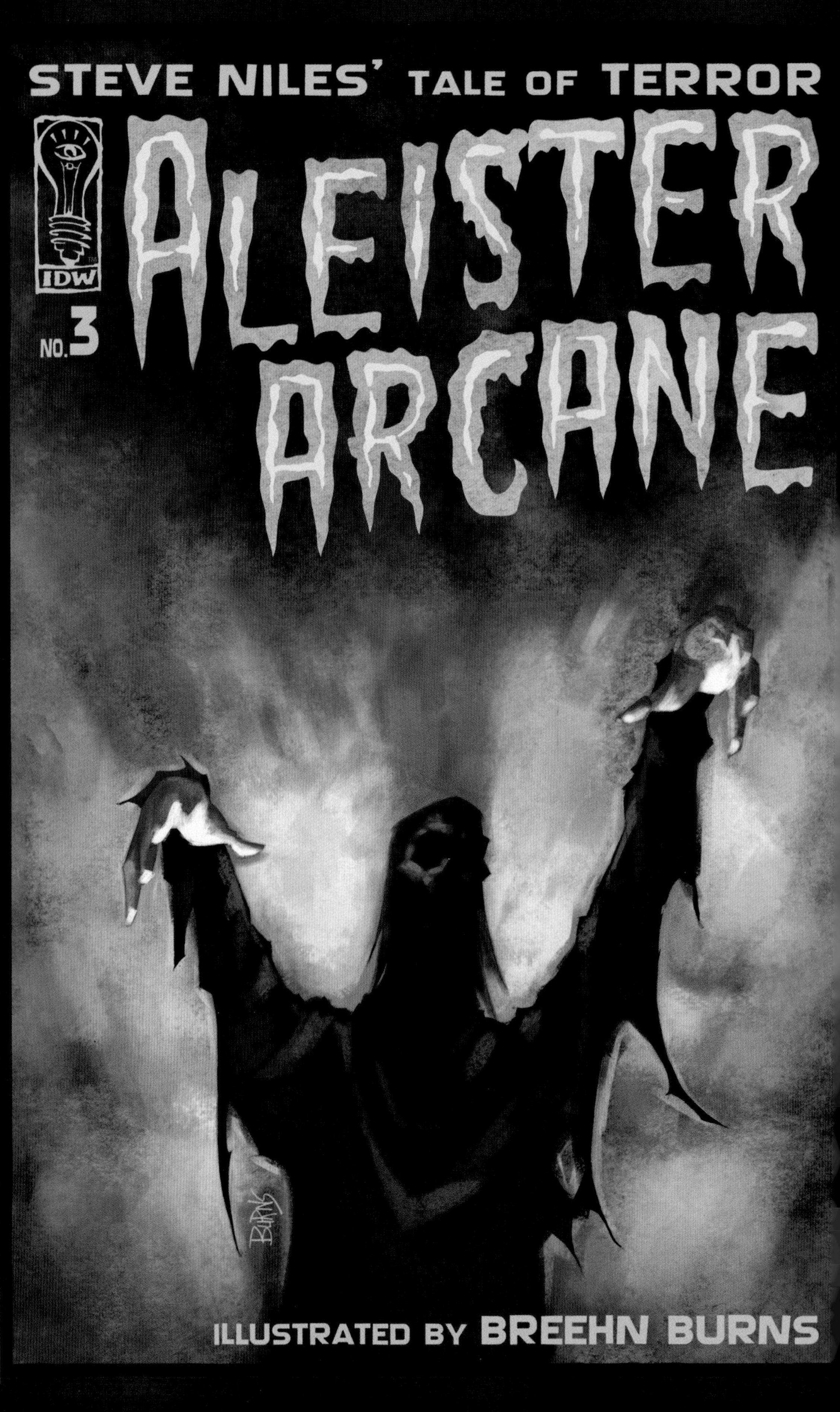
STEVE NILES' TALE OF TERROR
IDW
NO.3
ALEISTER
ARCANE
BURNS
ILLUSTRATED BY BREEHN BURNS

GRAAAAR!

AHHHHHHH!

AHH!

QUIT MESSING AROUND, GUYS. WE HAVE A LOT OF WORK TO DO.

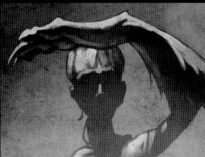

SLAMM!

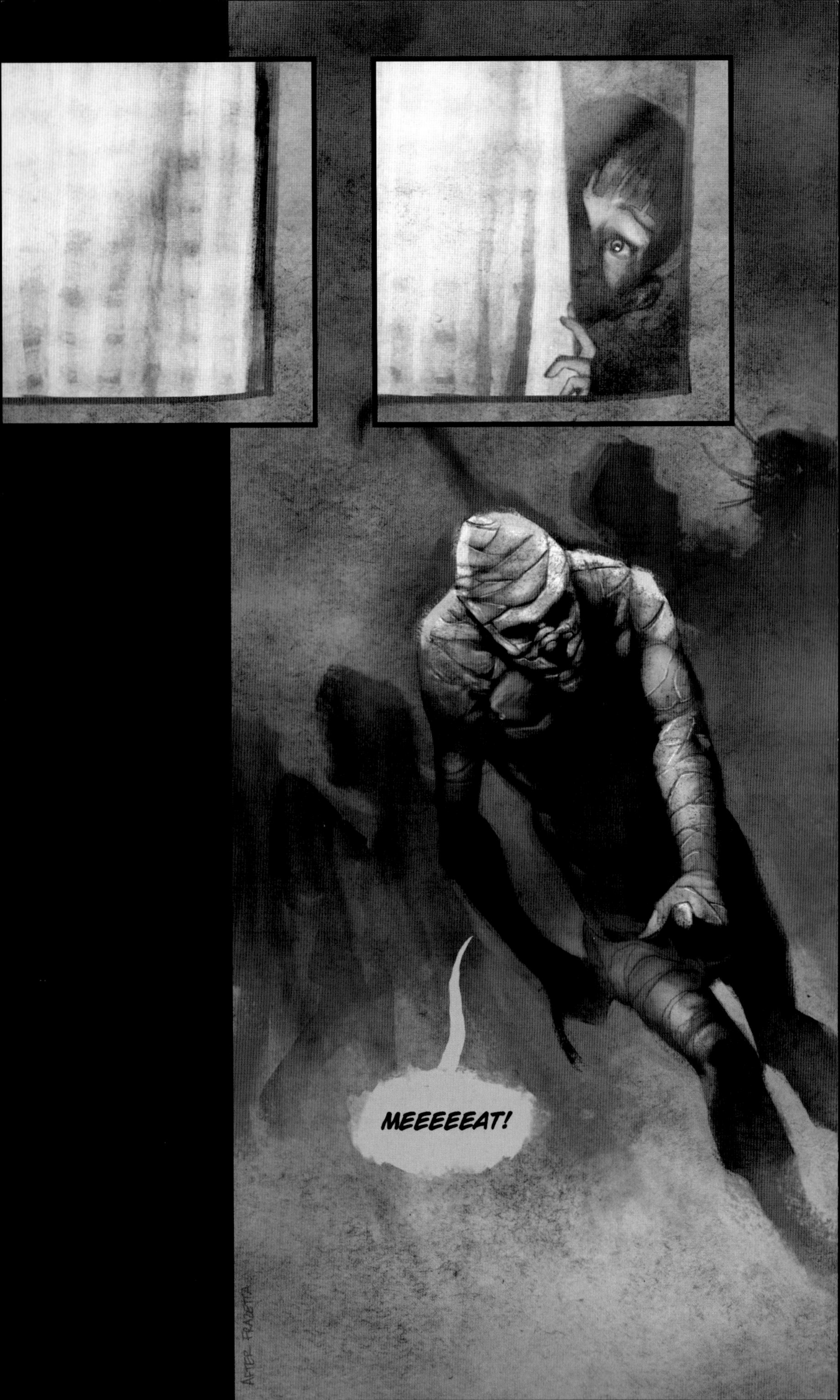
MEEEEEAT!

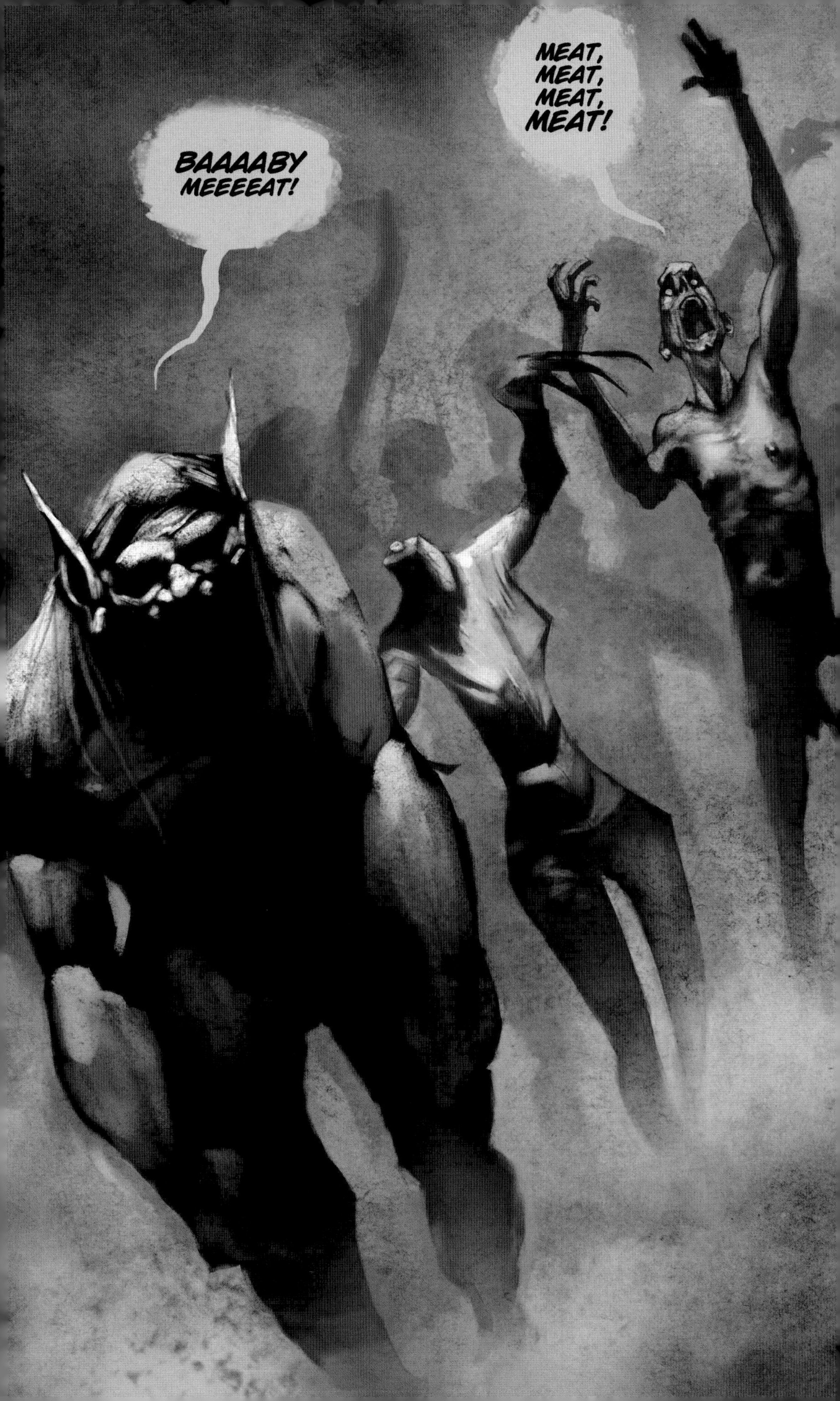
MEAT, MEAT, MEAT, MEAT!
BAAAABY MEEEEAT!

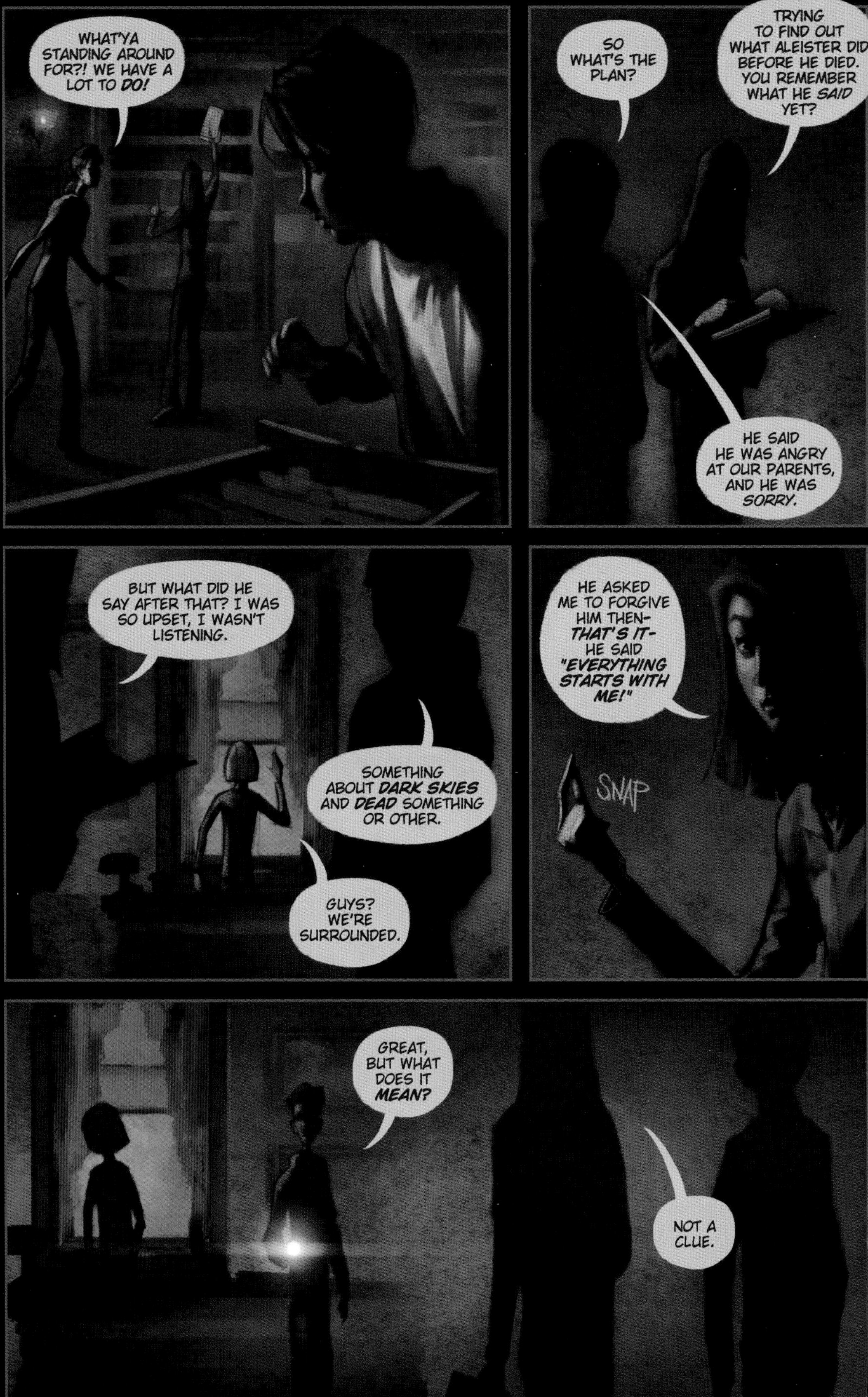
WHAT'YA STANDING AROUND FOR?! WE HAVE A LOT TO *DO!*
SO WHAT'S THE PLAN?
TRYING TO FIND OUT WHAT ALEISTER DID BEFORE HE DIED. YOU REMEMBER WHAT HE *SAID* YET?
HE SAID HE WAS ANGRY AT OUR PARENTS, AND HE WAS *SORRY.*
BUT WHAT DID HE SAY AFTER THAT? I WAS SO UPSET, I WASN'T LISTENING.
SOMETHING ABOUT ***DARK SKIES*** AND ***DEAD*** SOMETHING OR OTHER.
GUYS? WE'RE SURROUNDED.
HE ASKED ME TO FORGIVE HIM THEN- ***THAT'S IT-*** HE SAID ***"EVERYTHING STARTS WITH ME!"***
SNAP
GREAT, BUT WHAT DOES IT ***MEAN?***
NOT A CLUE.

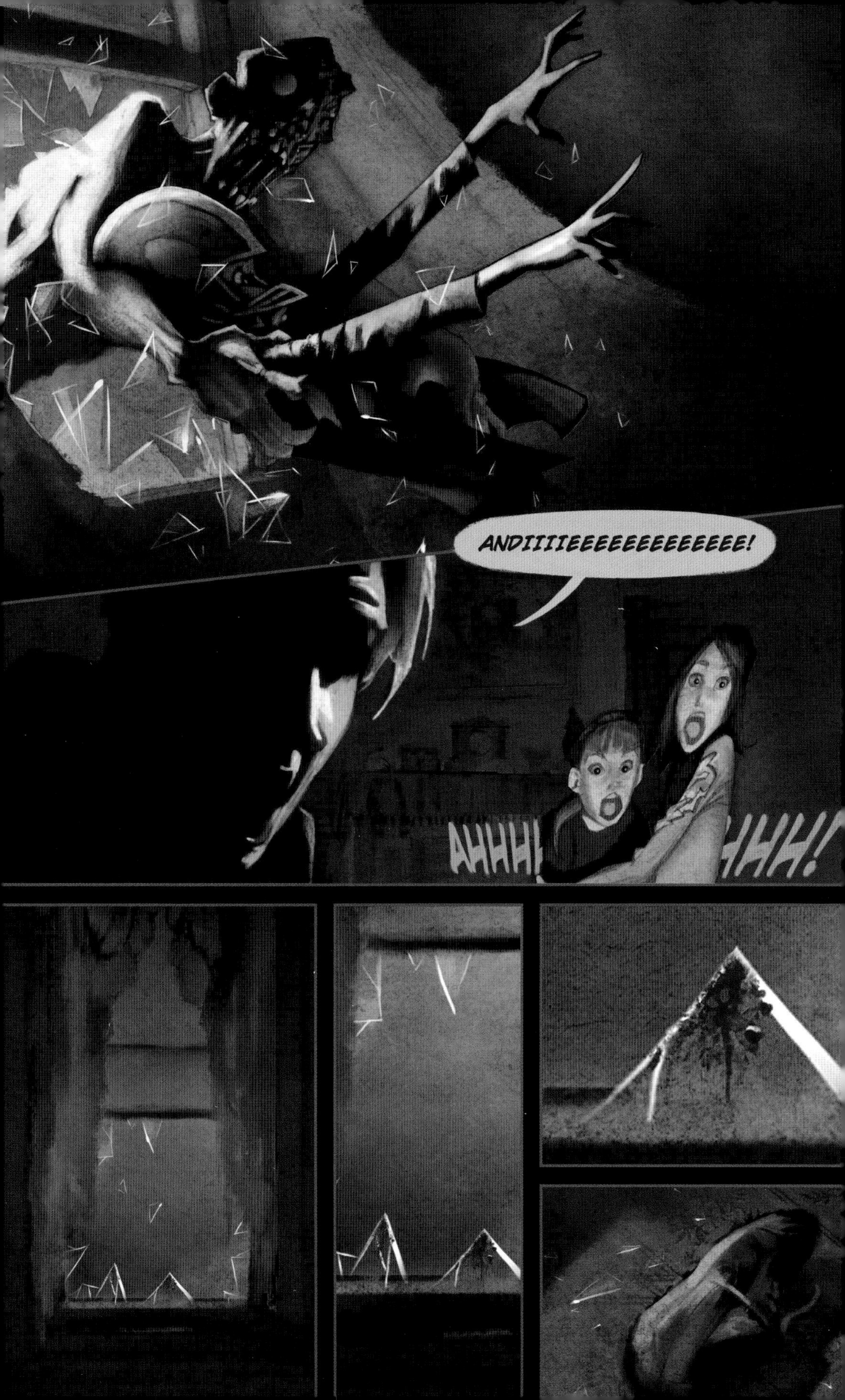
ANDIIIIEEEEEEEEEEEEEE!
AHHH HHH!

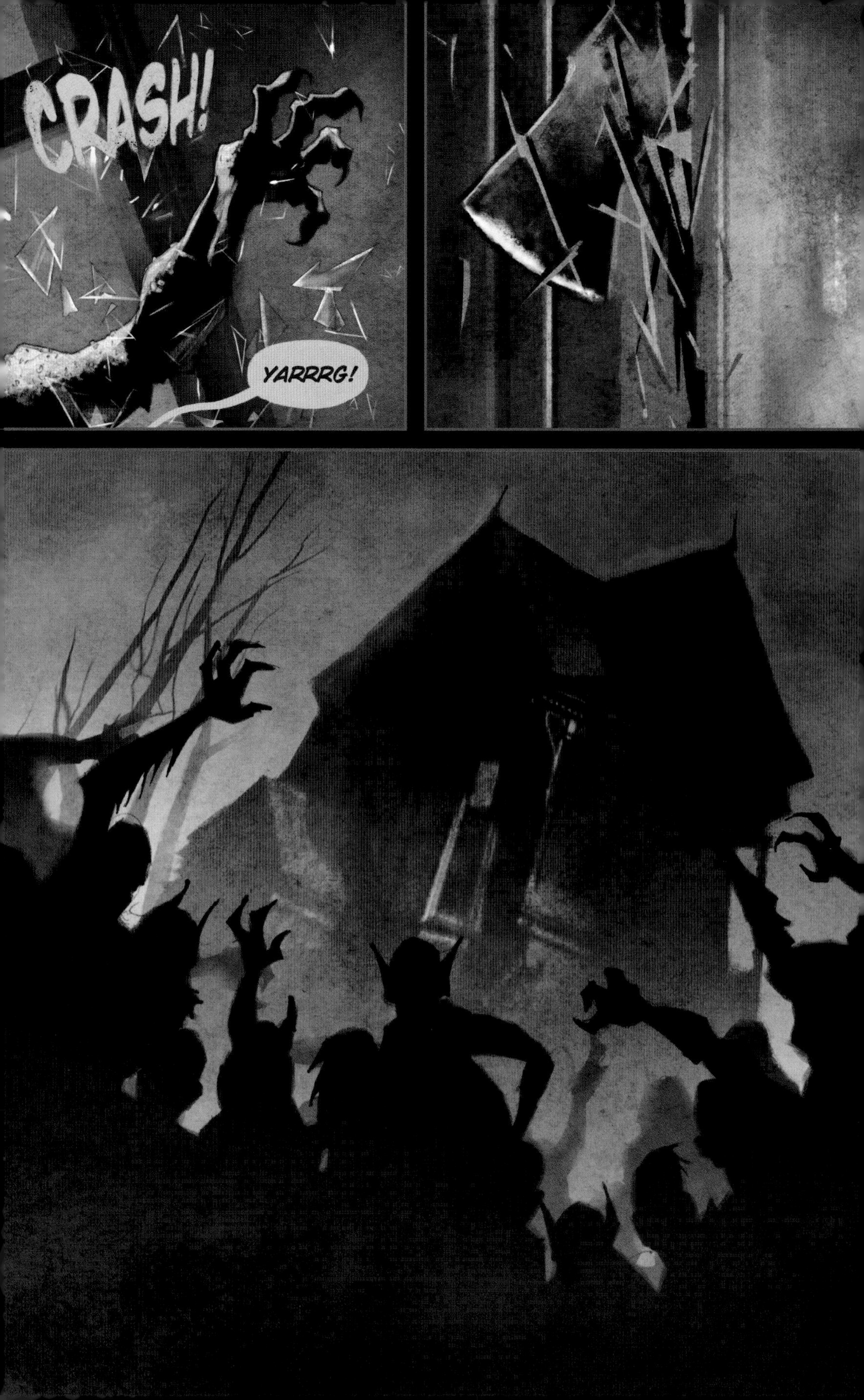
CRASH!
YARRRG!

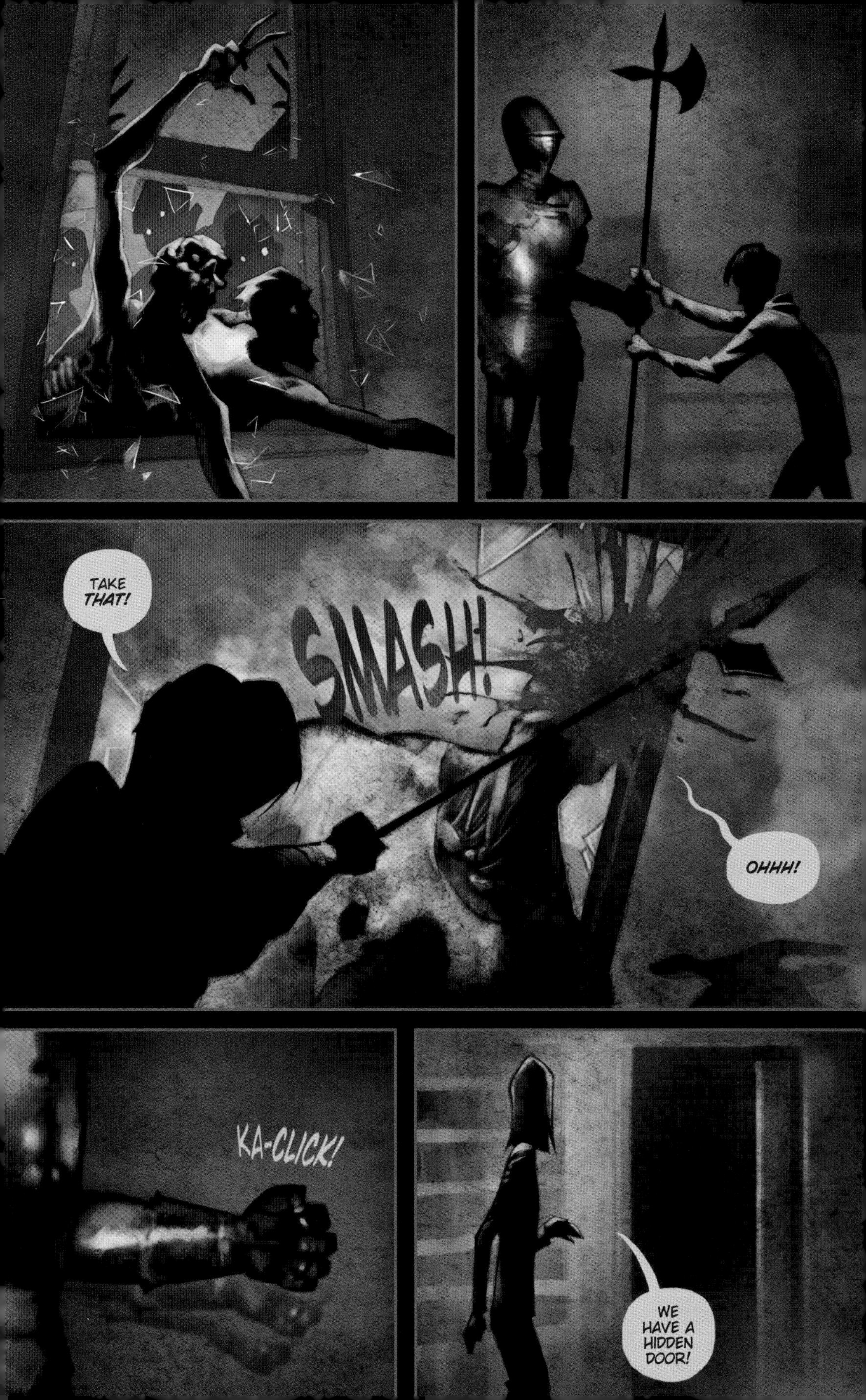
TAKE THAT!
SMASH!
OHHH!
KA-CLICK!
WE HAVE A HIDDEN DOOR!

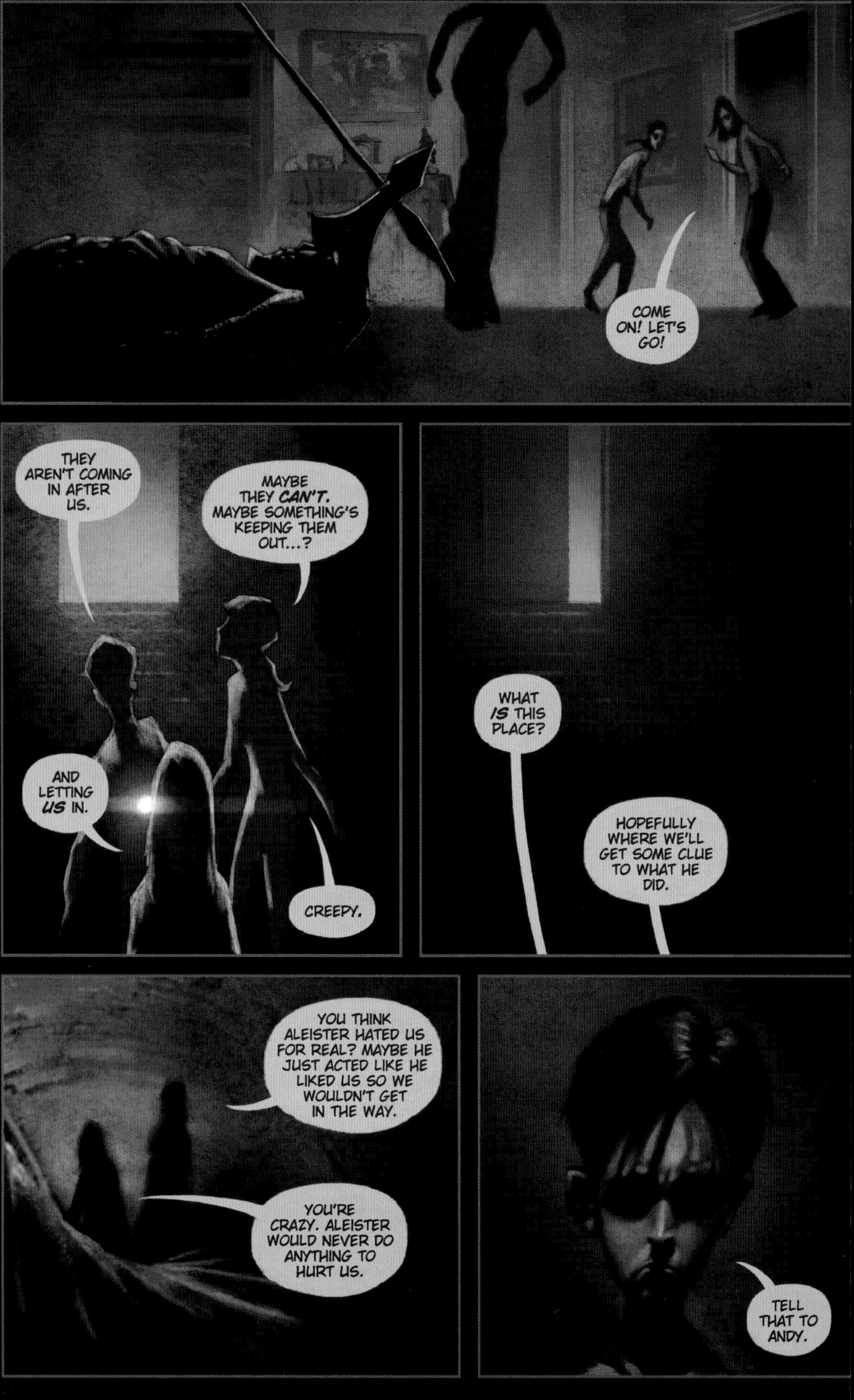

COME ON! LET'S GO!
THEY AREN'T COMING IN AFTER US.
MAYBE THEY CAN'T. MAYBE SOMETHING'S KEEPING THEM OUT...?
AND LETTING US IN.
CREEPY.
WHAT IS THIS PLACE?
HOPEFULLY WHERE WE'LL GET SOME CLUE TO WHAT HE DID.
YOU THINK ALEISTER HATED US FOR REAL? MAYBE HE JUST ACTED LIKE HE LIKED US SO WE WOULDN'T GET IN THE WAY.
YOU'RE CRAZY. ALEISTER WOULD NEVER DO ANYTHING TO HURT US.
TELL THAT TO ANDY.

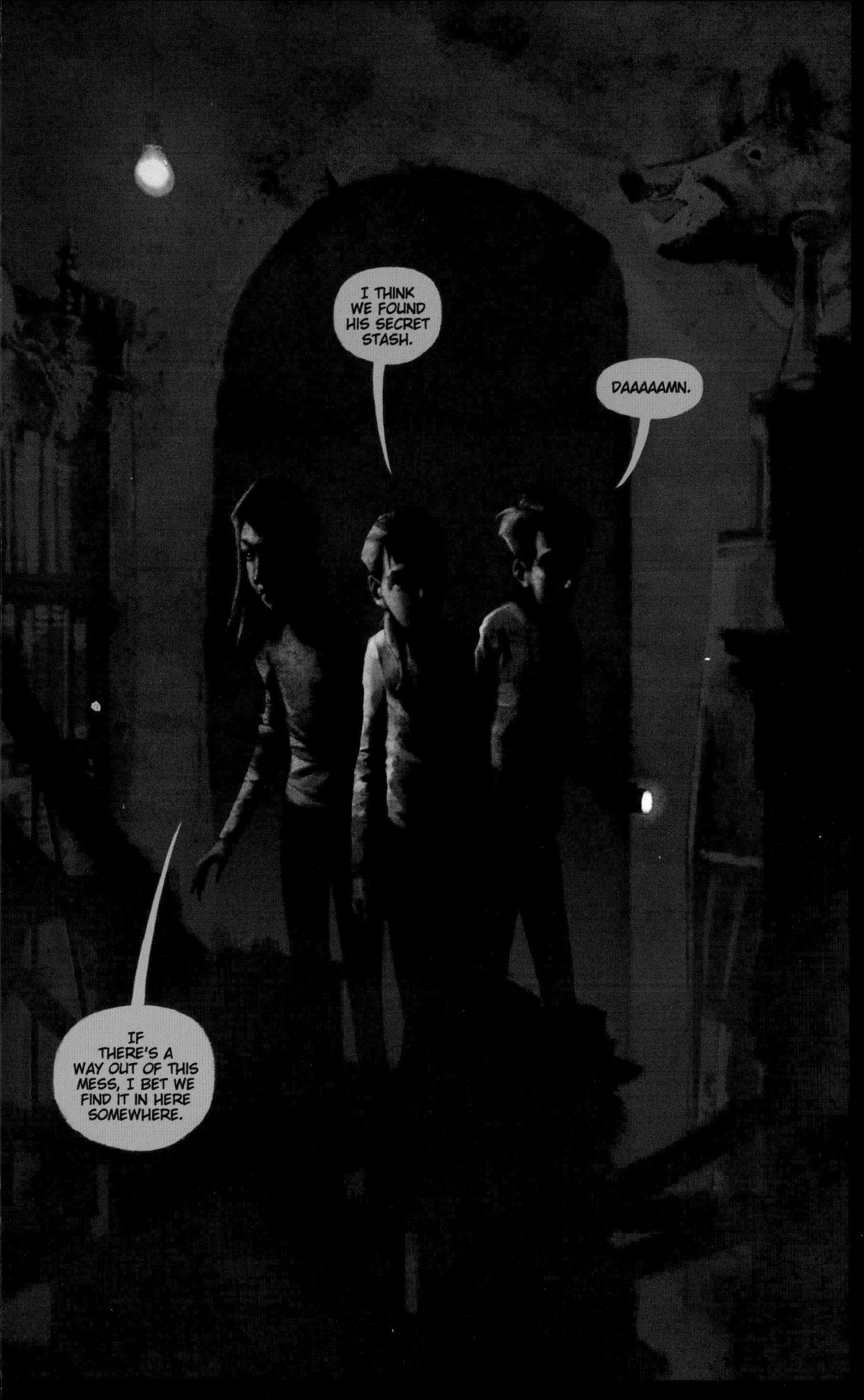
I THINK WE FOUND HIS SECRET STASH.
DAAAAAAMN.
IF THERE'S A WAY OUT OF THIS MESS, I BET WE FIND IT IN HERE SOMEWHERE.

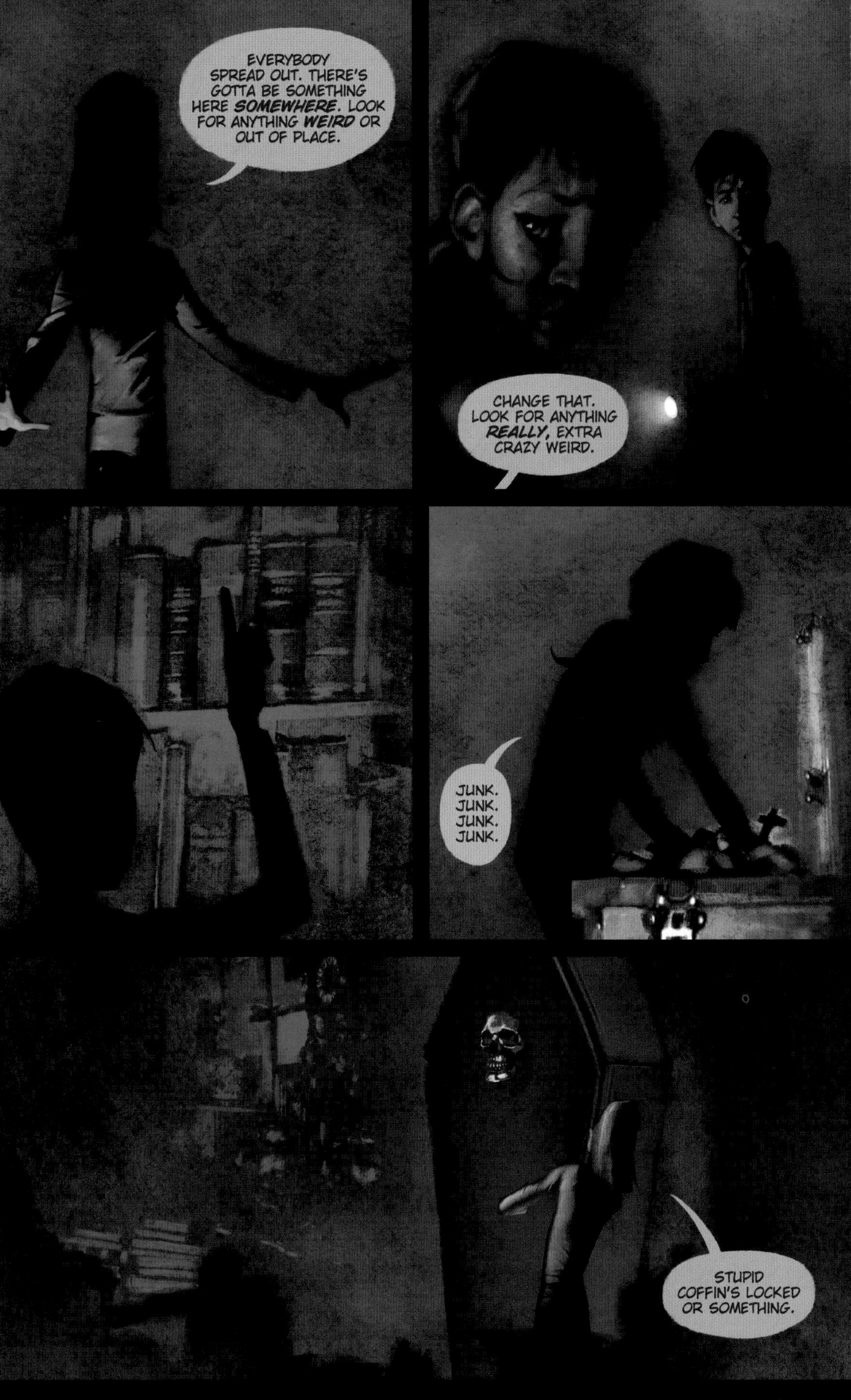
EVERYBODY SPREAD OUT. THERE'S GOTTA BE SOMETHING HERE SOMEWHERE. LOOK FOR ANYTHING WEIRD OR OUT OF PLACE.
CHANGE THAT. LOOK FOR ANYTHING REALLY, EXTRA CRAZY WEIRD.
JUNK. JUNK. JUNK. JUNK.
STUPID COFFIN'S LOCKED OR SOMETHING.

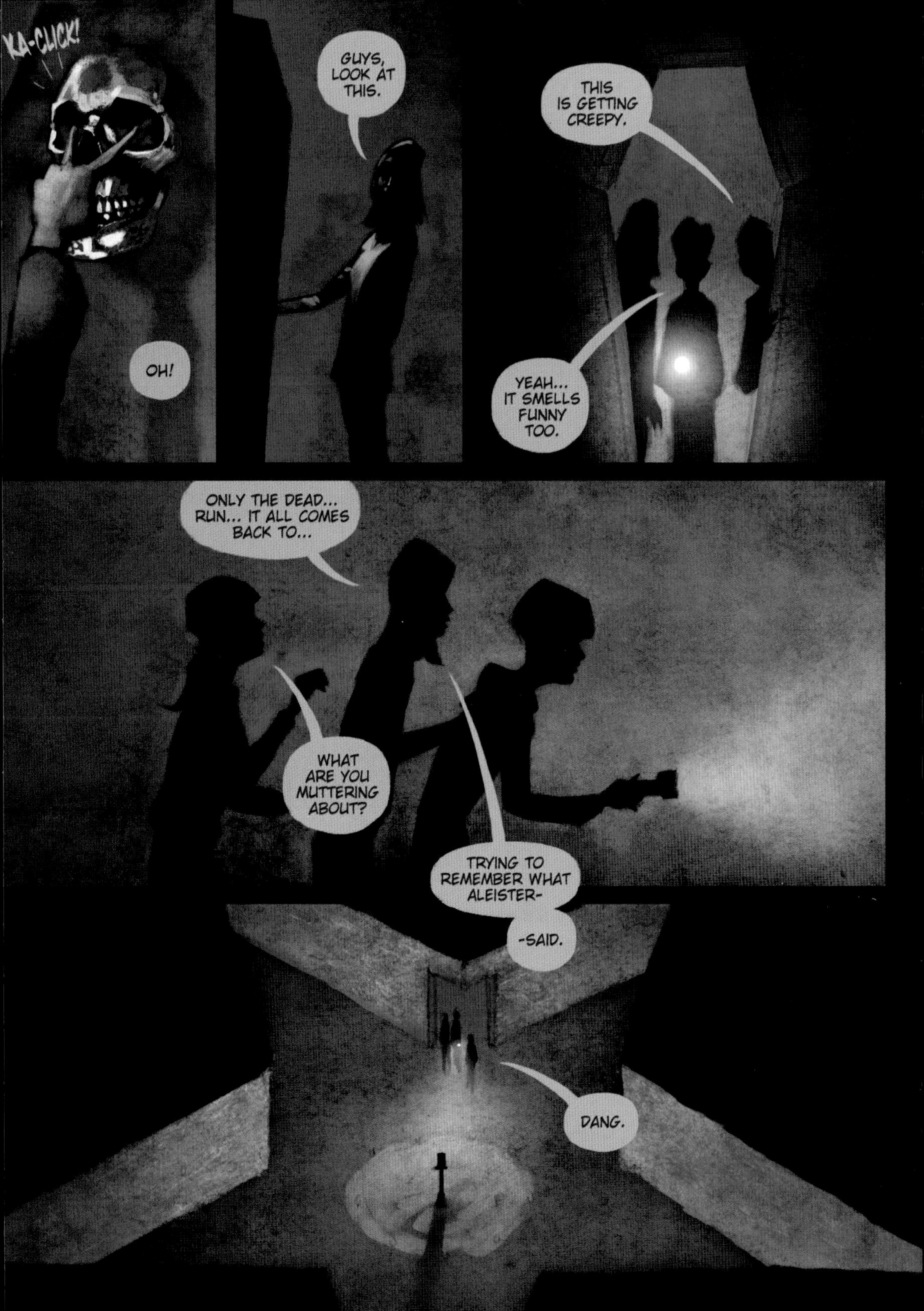
KA-CLICK!
OH!
GUYS, LOOK AT THIS.
THIS IS GETTING CREEPY.
YEAH... IT SMELLS FUNNY TOO.
ONLY THE DEAD... RUN... IT ALL COMES BACK TO...
WHAT ARE YOU MUTTERING ABOUT?
TRYING TO REMEMBER WHAT ALEISTER-
-SAID.
DANG.

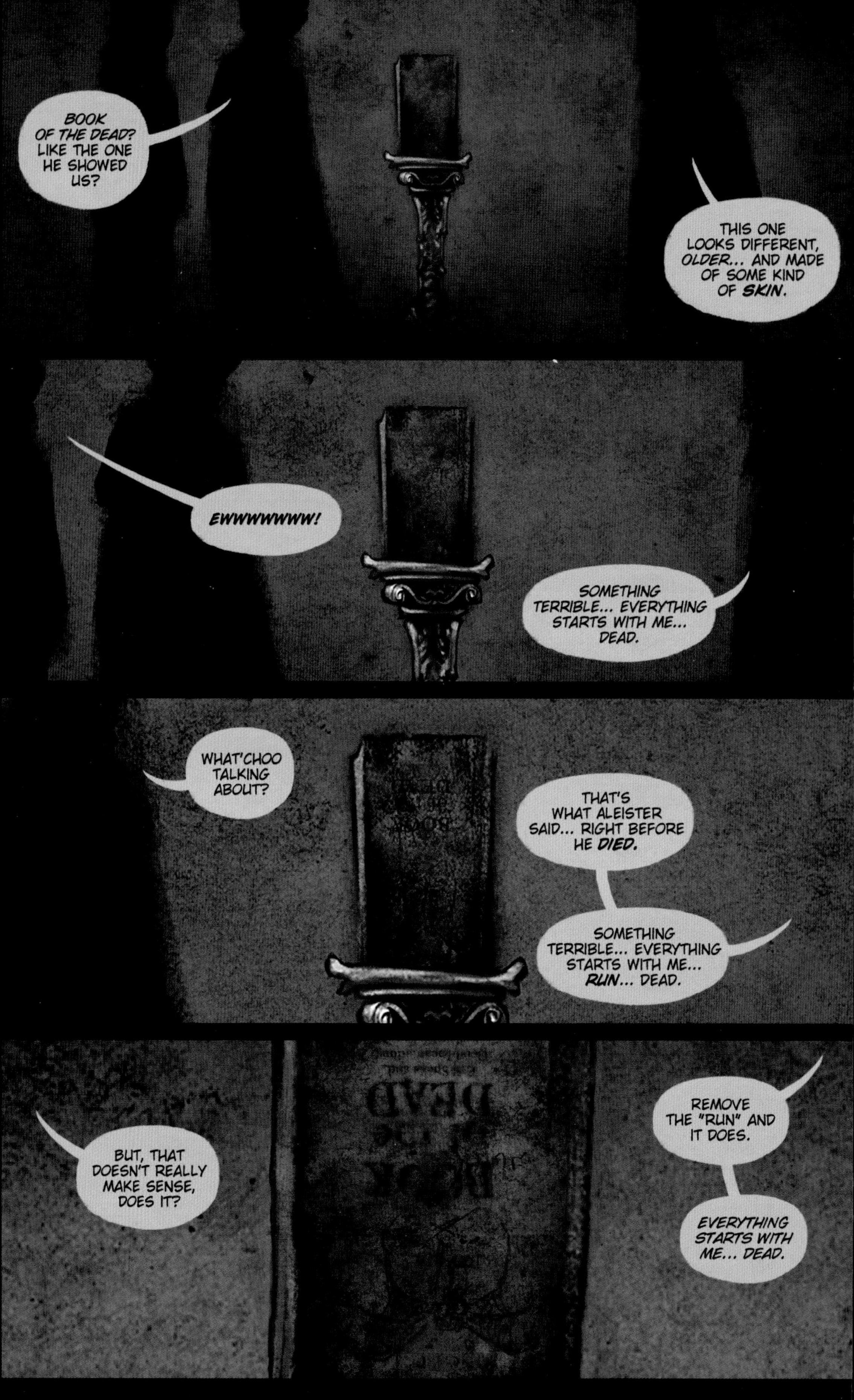
BOOK OF THE DEAD? LIKE THE ONE HE SHOWED US?
THIS ONE LOOKS DIFFERENT, OLDER... AND MADE OF SOME KIND OF SKIN.
EWWWWWWW!
SOMETHING TERRIBLE... EVERYTHING STARTS WITH ME... DEAD.
WHAT'CHOO TALKING ABOUT?
THAT'S WHAT ALEISTER SAID... RIGHT BEFORE HE DIED.
SOMETHING TERRIBLE... EVERYTHING STARTS WITH ME... RUN... DEAD.
BUT, THAT DOESN'T REALLY MAKE SENSE, DOES IT?
REMOVE THE "RUN" AND IT DOES.
EVERYTHING STARTS WITH ME... DEAD.

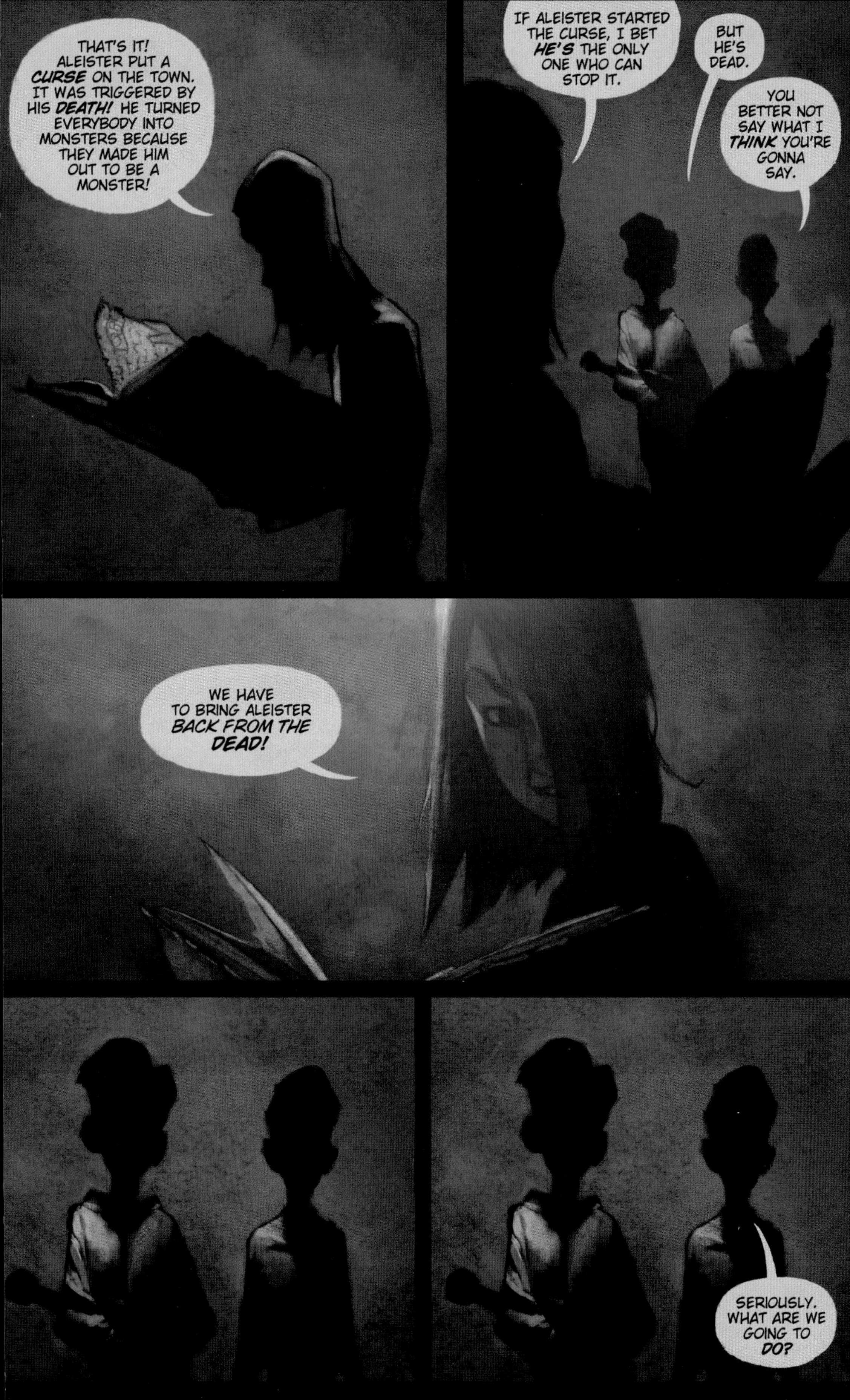
THAT'S IT! ALEISTER PUT A CURSE ON THE TOWN. IT WAS TRIGGERED BY HIS DEATH! HE TURNED EVERYBODY INTO MONSTERS BECAUSE THEY MADE HIM OUT TO BE A MONSTER!
IF ALEISTER STARTED THE CURSE, I BET HE'S THE ONLY ONE WHO CAN STOP IT.
BUT HE'S DEAD.
YOU BETTER NOT SAY WHAT I THINK YOU'RE GONNA SAY.
WE HAVE TO BRING ALEISTER BACK FROM THE DEAD!
SERIOUSLY. WHAT ARE WE GOING TO DO?

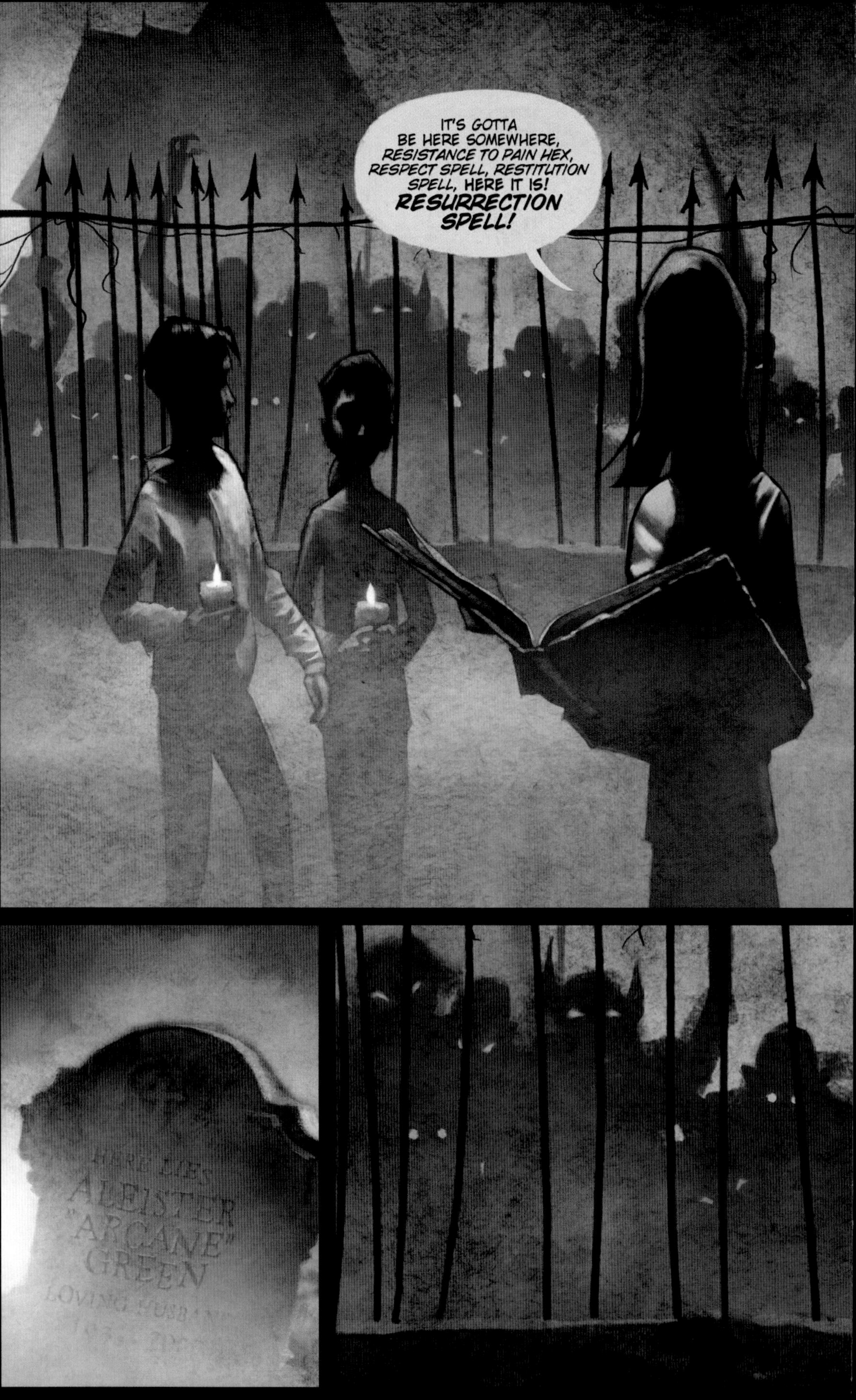
IT'S GOTTA BE HERE SOMEWHERE, *RESISTANCE TO PAIN HEX, RESPECT SPELL, RESTITUTION SPELL*, HERE IT IS! ***RESURRECTION SPELL!***
ALEISTER "ARCANE" GREEN

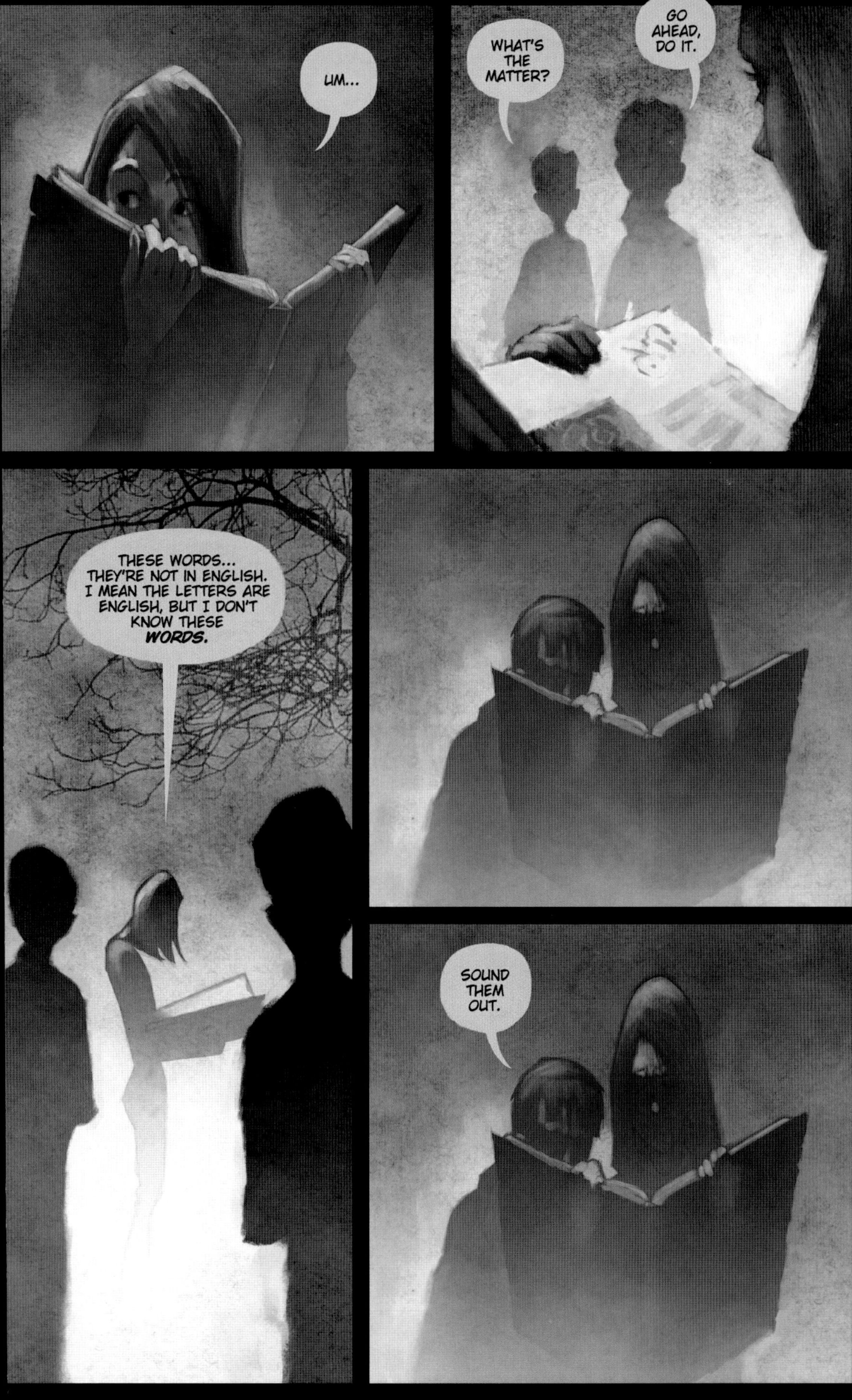
UM...
WHAT'S THE MATTER?
GO AHEAD, DO IT.
THESE WORDS... THEY'RE NOT IN ENGLISH. I MEAN THE LETTERS ARE ENGLISH, BUT I DON'T KNOW THESE **WORDS.**
SOUND THEM OUT.

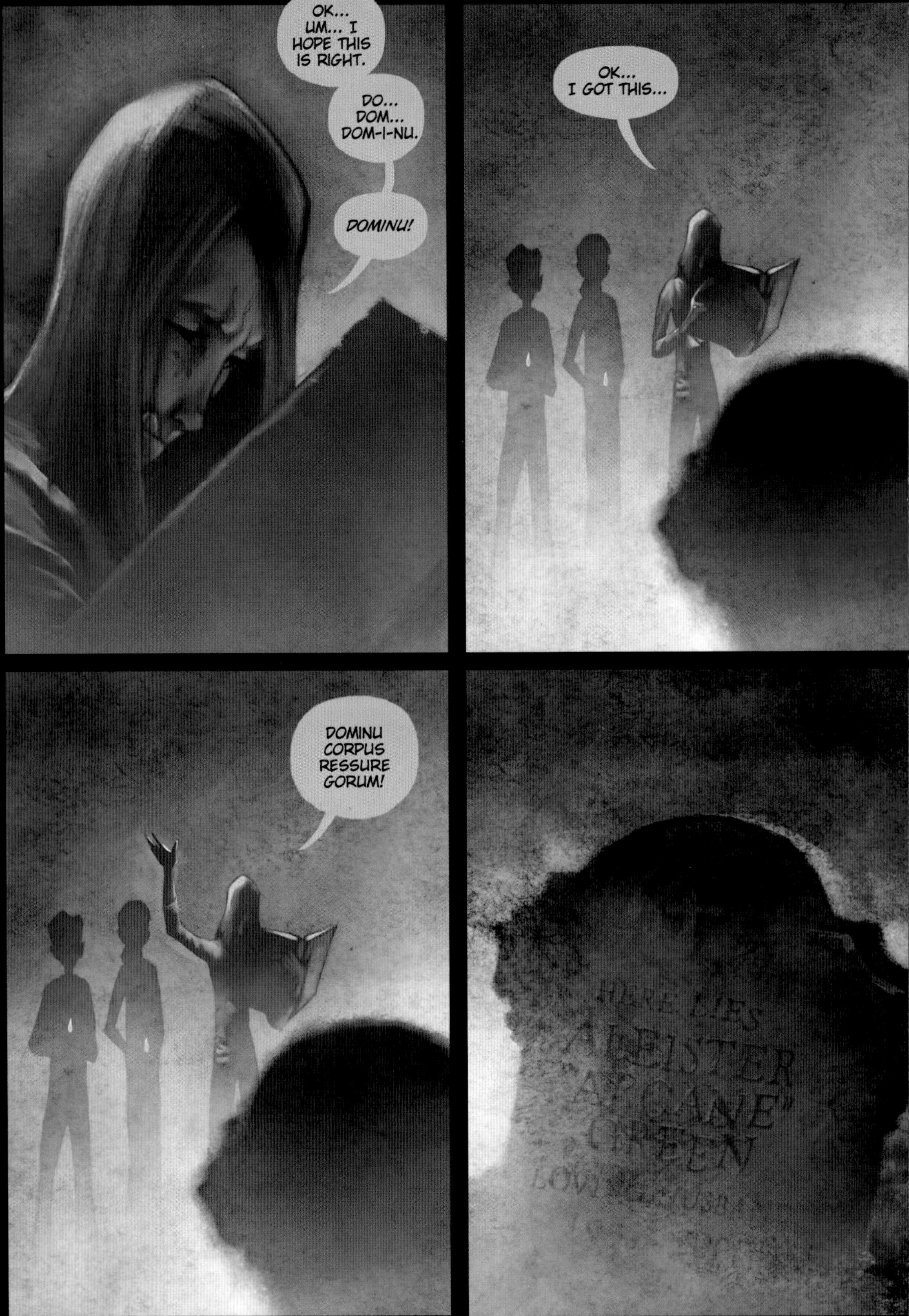
OK... UM... I HOPE THIS IS RIGHT.
DO... DOM... DOM-I-NU.
DOMINU!
OK... I GOT THIS...
DOMINU CORPUS RESSURE GORUM!

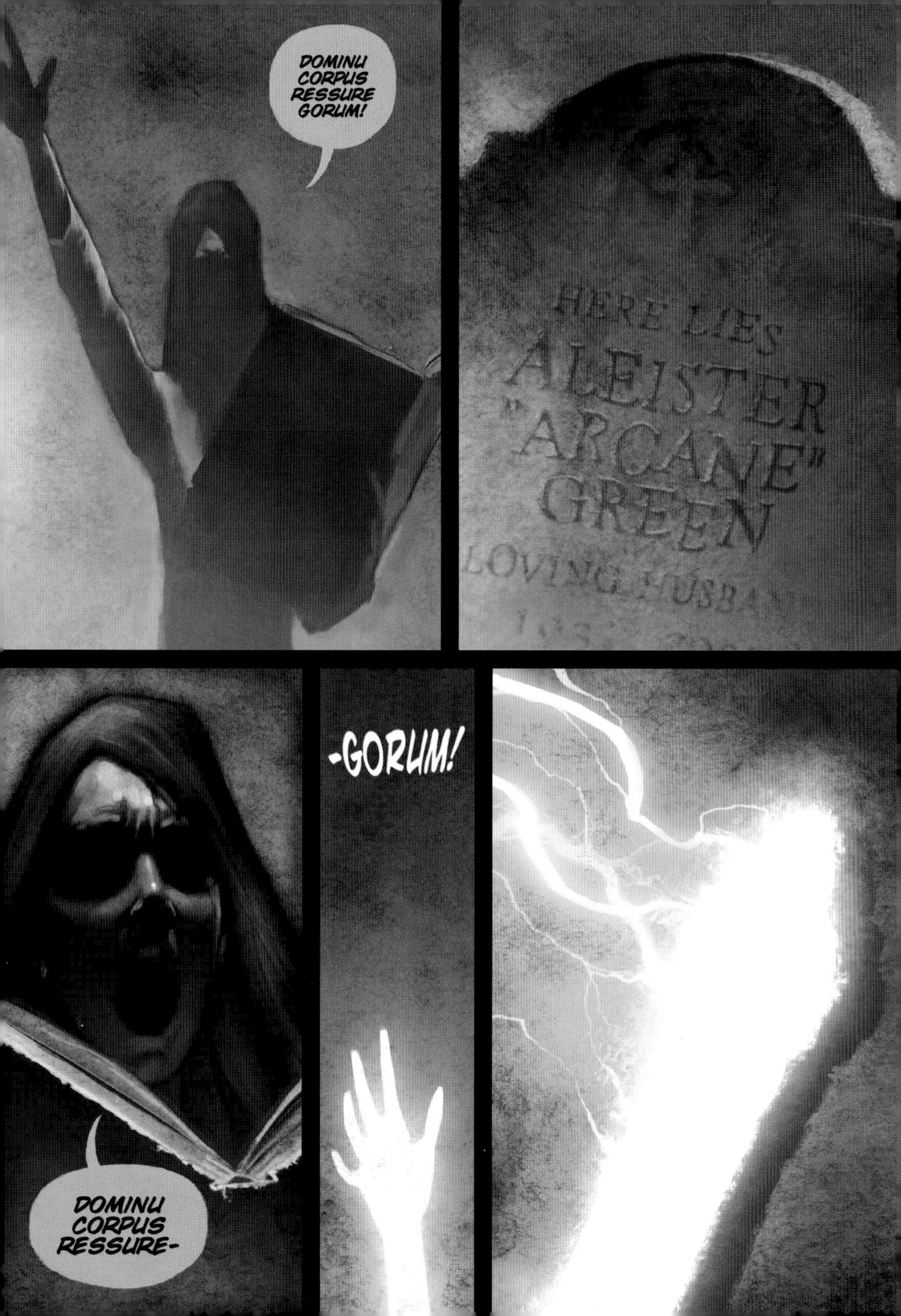
DOMINU CORPUS RESSURE GORUM!
HERE LIES
ALEISTER
"ARCANE"
GREEN
LOVING
DOMINU CORPUS RESSURE-
-GORUM!

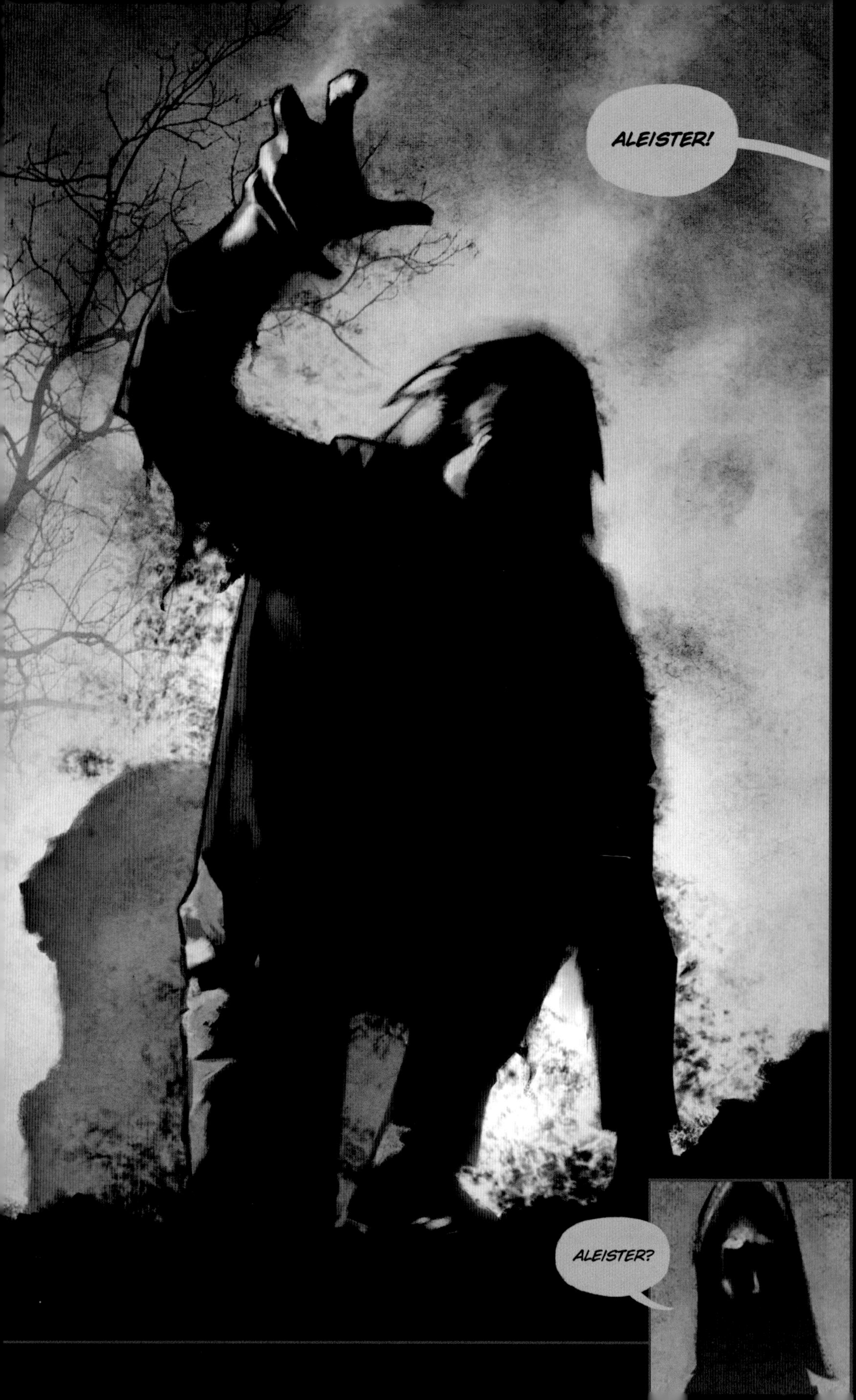
ALEISTER!
ALEISTER?

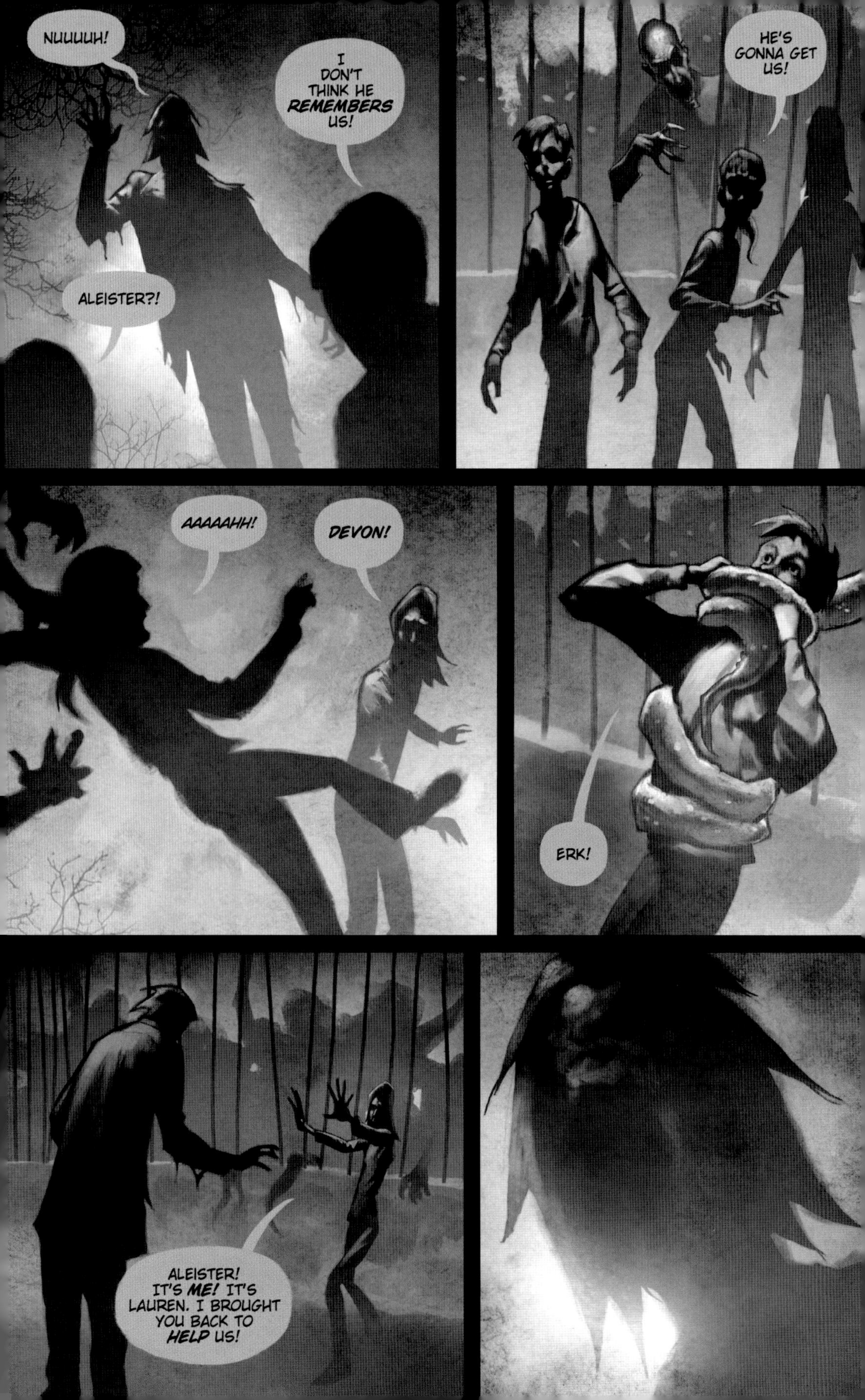
NUUUUH!
I DON'T THINK HE REMEMBERS US!
ALEISTER?!
HE'S GONNA GET US!
AAAAAHH!
DEVON!
ERK!
ALEISTER! IT'S ME! IT'S LAUREN. I BROUGHT YOU BACK TO HELP US!

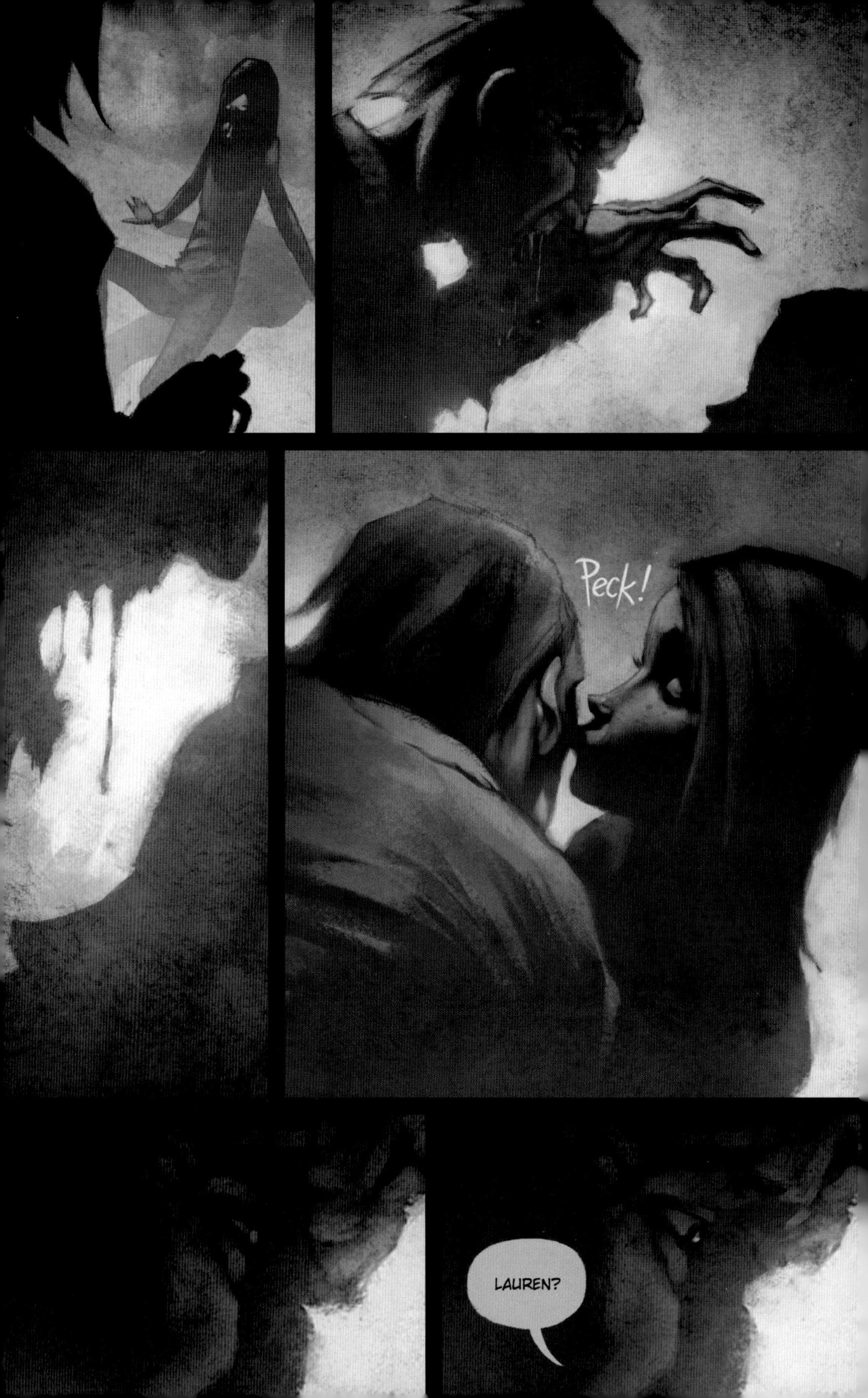
Peck!
LAUREN?

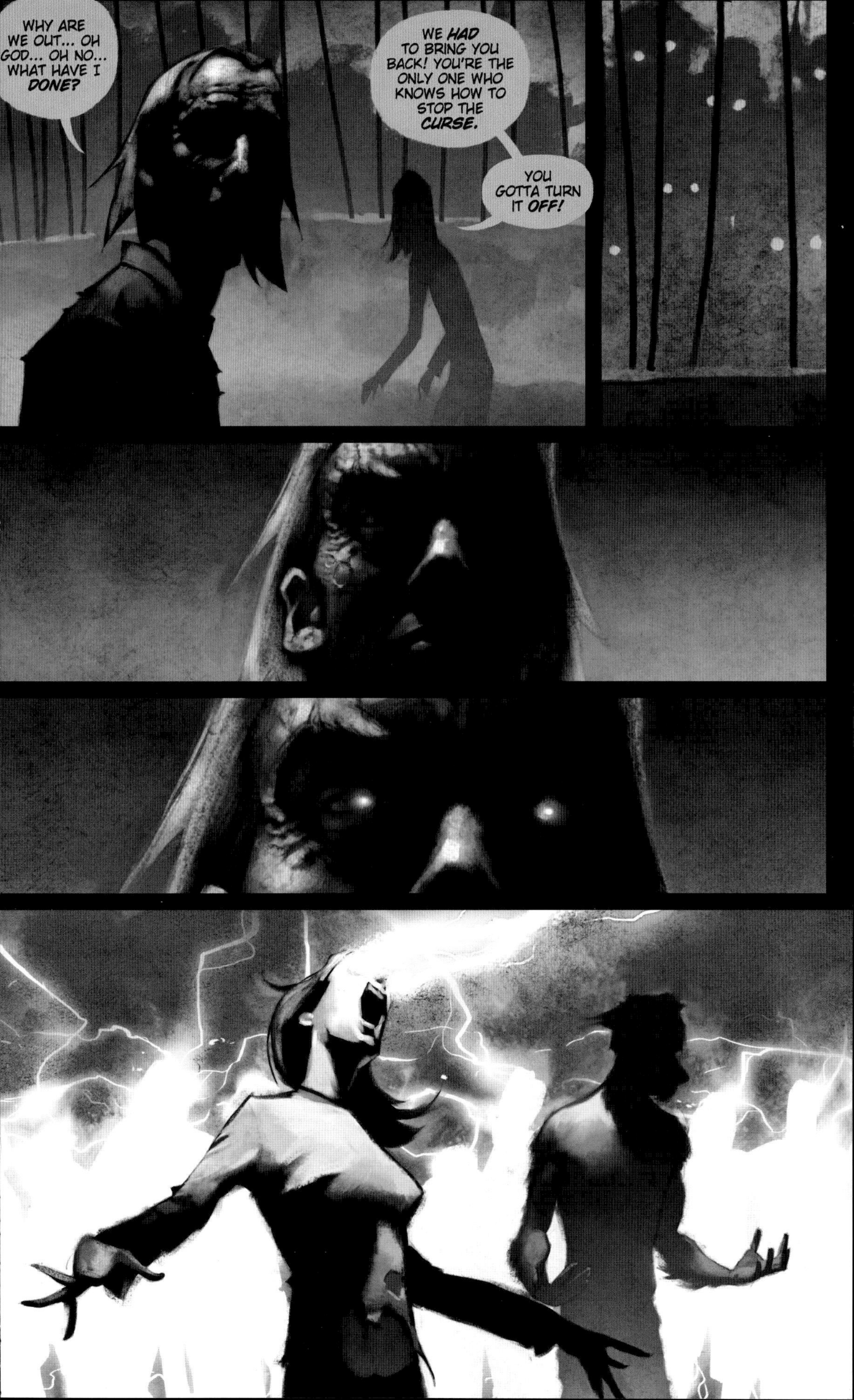
WHY ARE WE OUT... OH GOD... OH NO... WHAT HAVE I DONE?
WE HAD TO BRING YOU BACK! YOU'RE THE ONLY ONE WHO KNOWS HOW TO STOP THE CURSE.
YOU GOTTA TURN IT OFF!

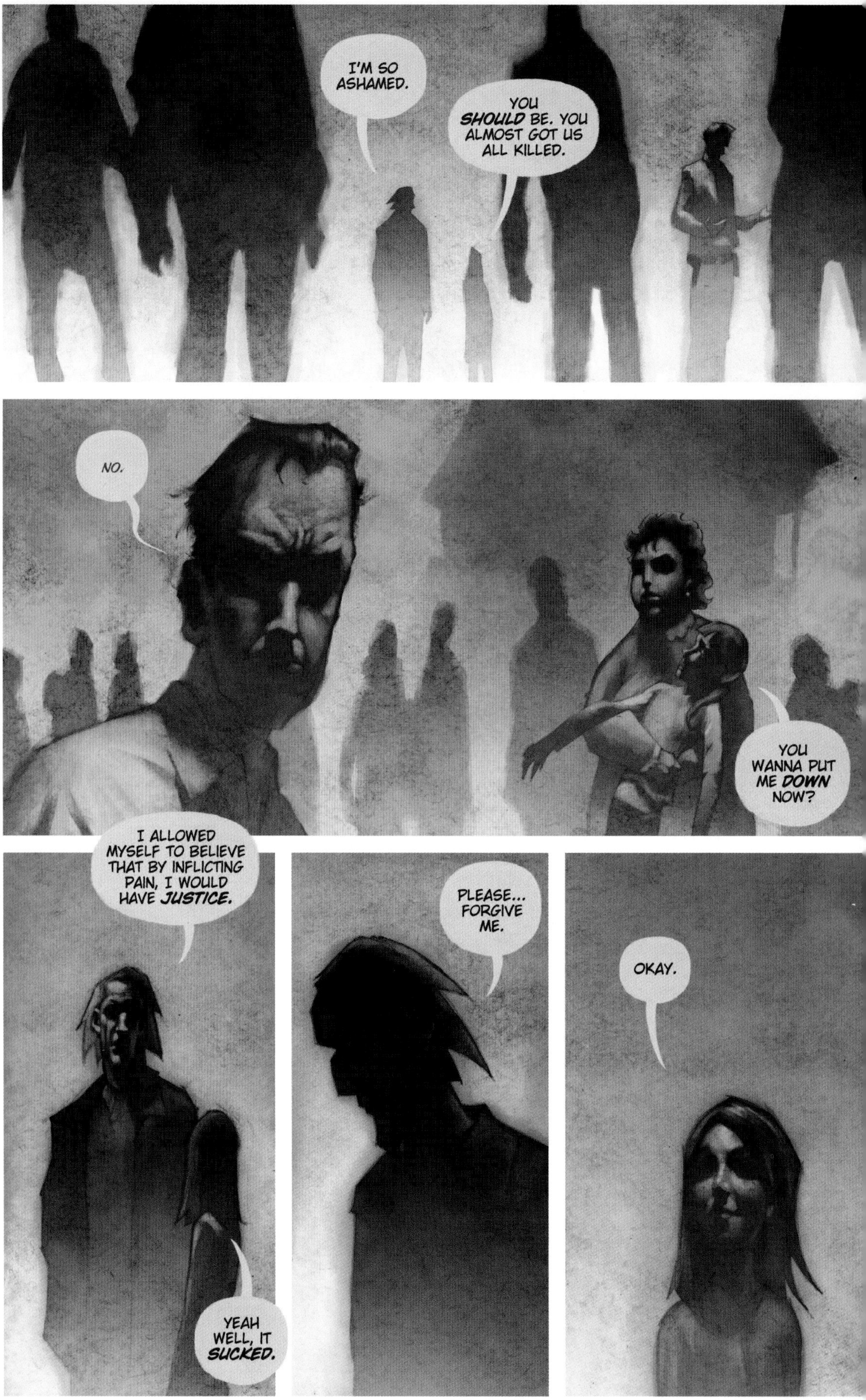
I'M SO ASHAMED.
YOU SHOULD BE. YOU ALMOST GOT US ALL KILLED.
NO.
YOU WANNA PUT ME DOWN NOW?
I ALLOWED MYSELF TO BELIEVE THAT BY INFLICTING PAIN, I WOULD HAVE JUSTICE.
YEAH WELL, IT SUCKED.
PLEASE... FORGIVE ME.
OKAY.

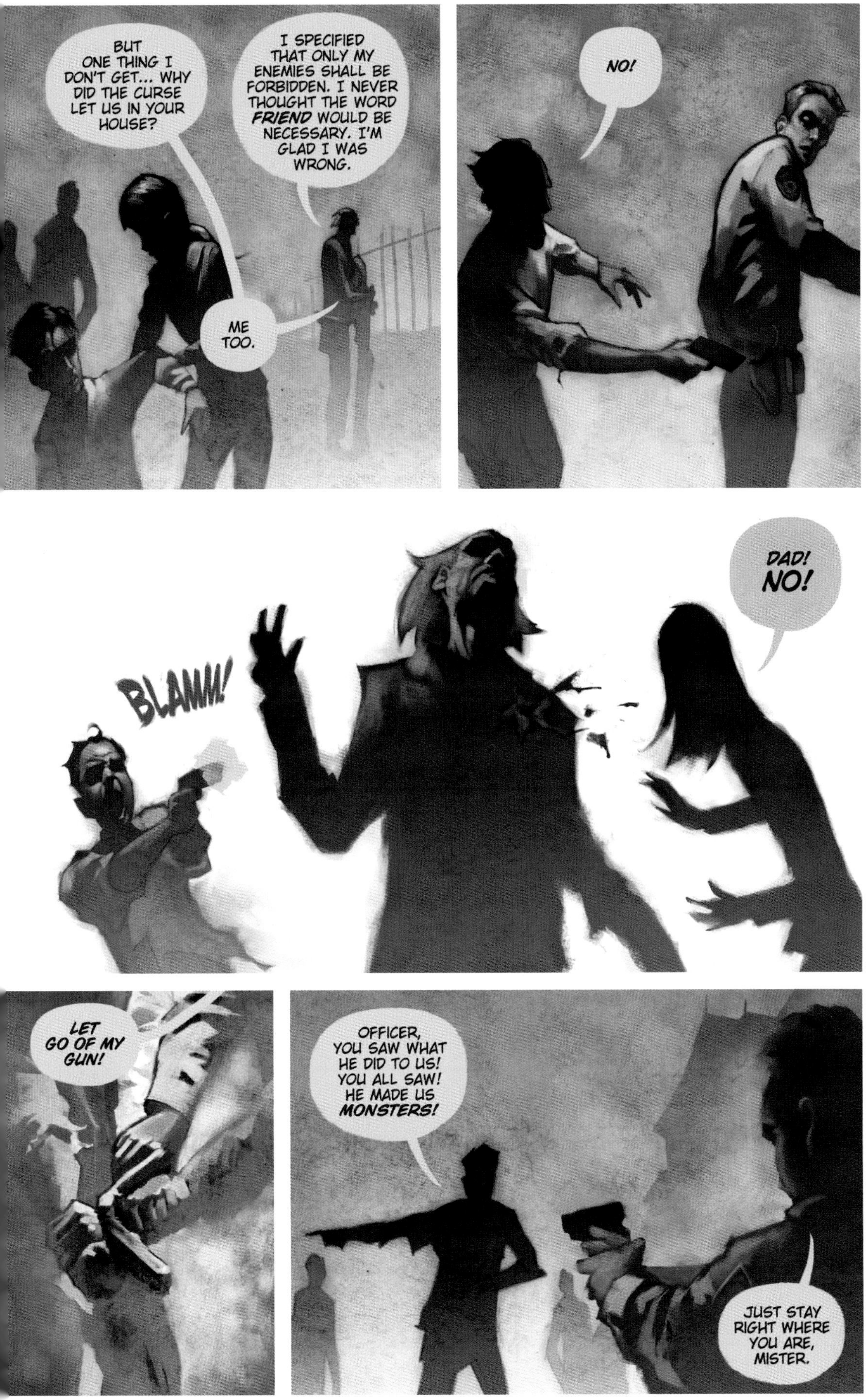
BUT ONE THING I DON'T GET... WHY DID THE CURSE LET US IN YOUR HOUSE?
I SPECIFIED THAT ONLY MY ENEMIES SHALL BE FORBIDDEN. I NEVER THOUGHT THE WORD **FRIEND** WOULD BE NECESSARY. I'M GLAD I WAS WRONG.
ME TOO.
NO!
BLAMM!
DAD! NO!
LET GO OF MY GUN!
OFFICER, YOU SAW WHAT HE DID TO US! YOU ALL SAW! HE MADE US **MONSTERS!**
JUST STAY RIGHT WHERE YOU ARE, MISTER.

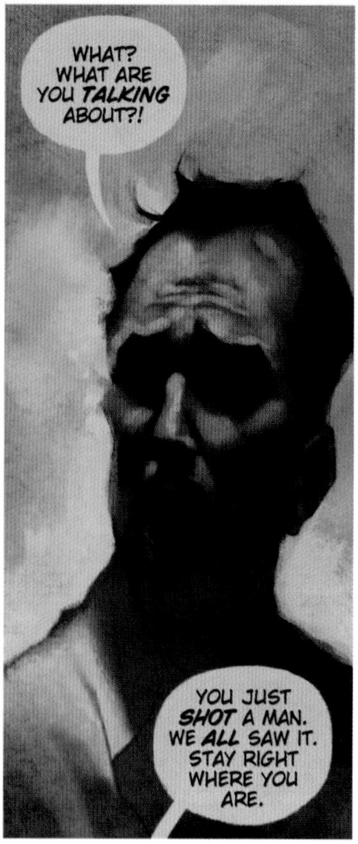
WHAT? WHAT ARE YOU *TALKING* ABOUT?!
YOU JUST *SHOT* A MAN. WE *ALL* SAW IT. STAY RIGHT WHERE YOU ARE.

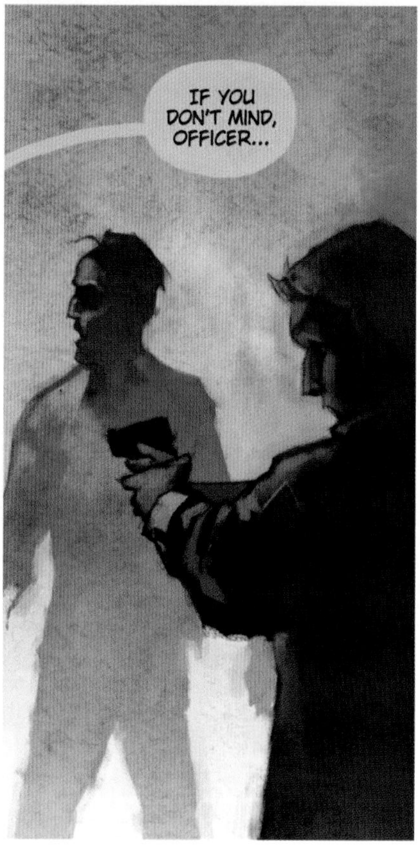
IF YOU DON'T MIND, OFFICER...

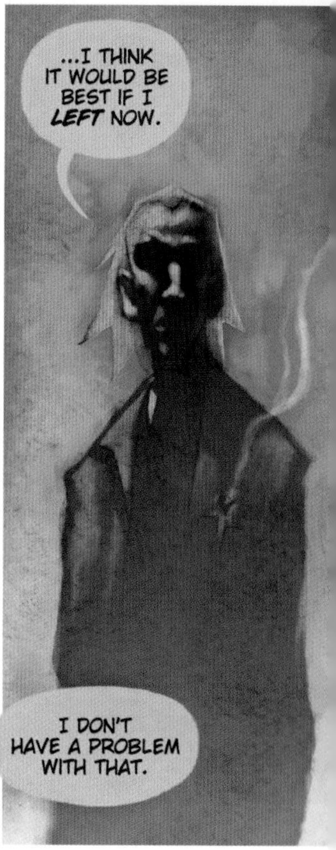
...I THINK IT WOULD BE BEST IF I *LEFT* NOW.
I DON'T HAVE A PROBLEM WITH THAT.

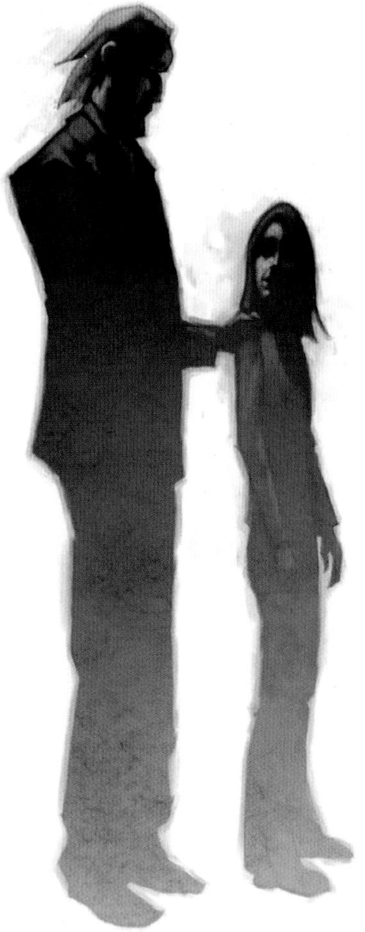

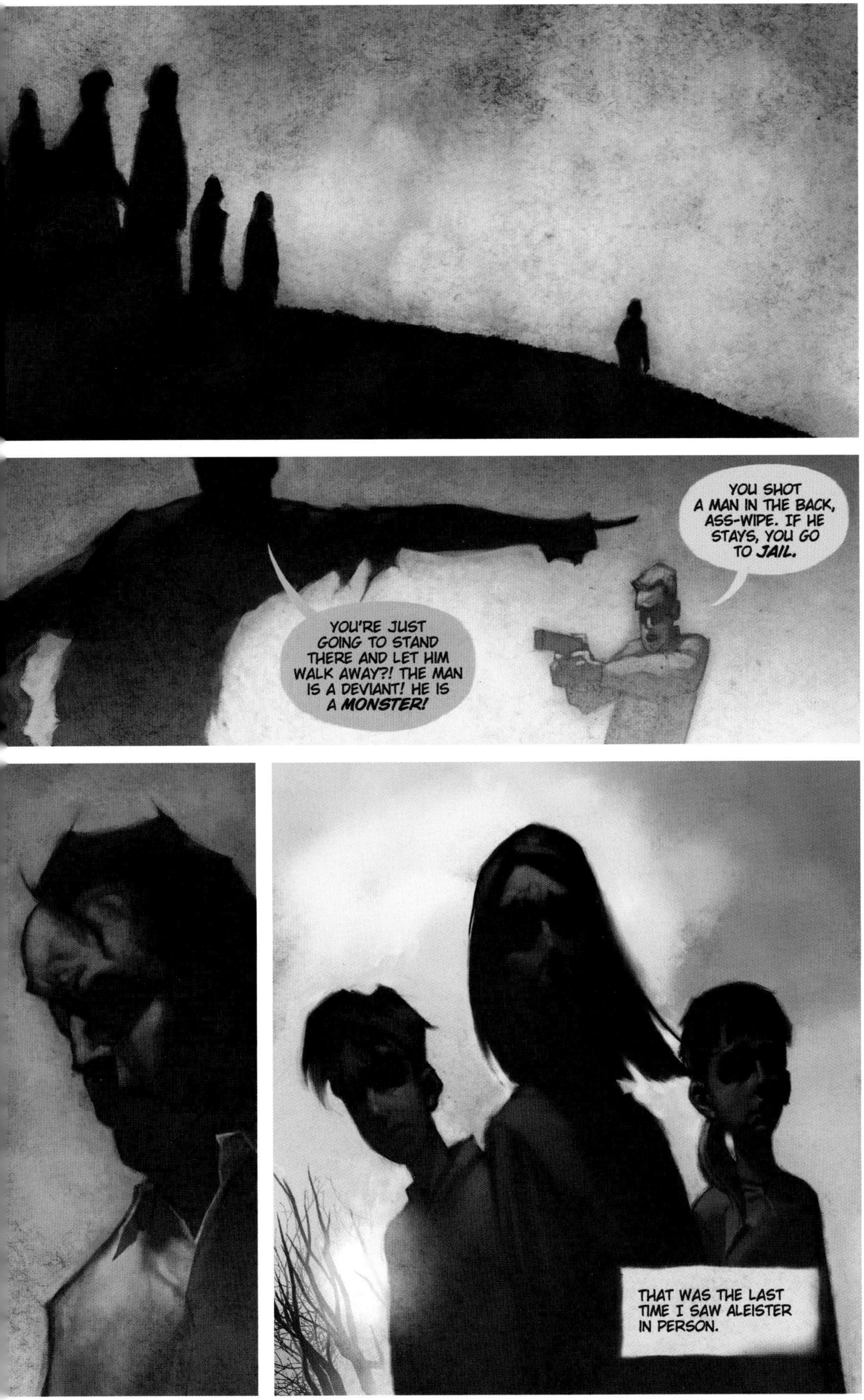
YOU'RE JUST GOING TO STAND THERE AND LET HIM WALK AWAY?! THE MAN IS A DEVIANT! HE IS A *MONSTER!*
YOU SHOT A MAN IN THE BACK, ASS-WIPE. IF HE STAYS, YOU GO TO *JAIL.*
THAT WAS THE LAST TIME I SAW ALEISTER IN PERSON.

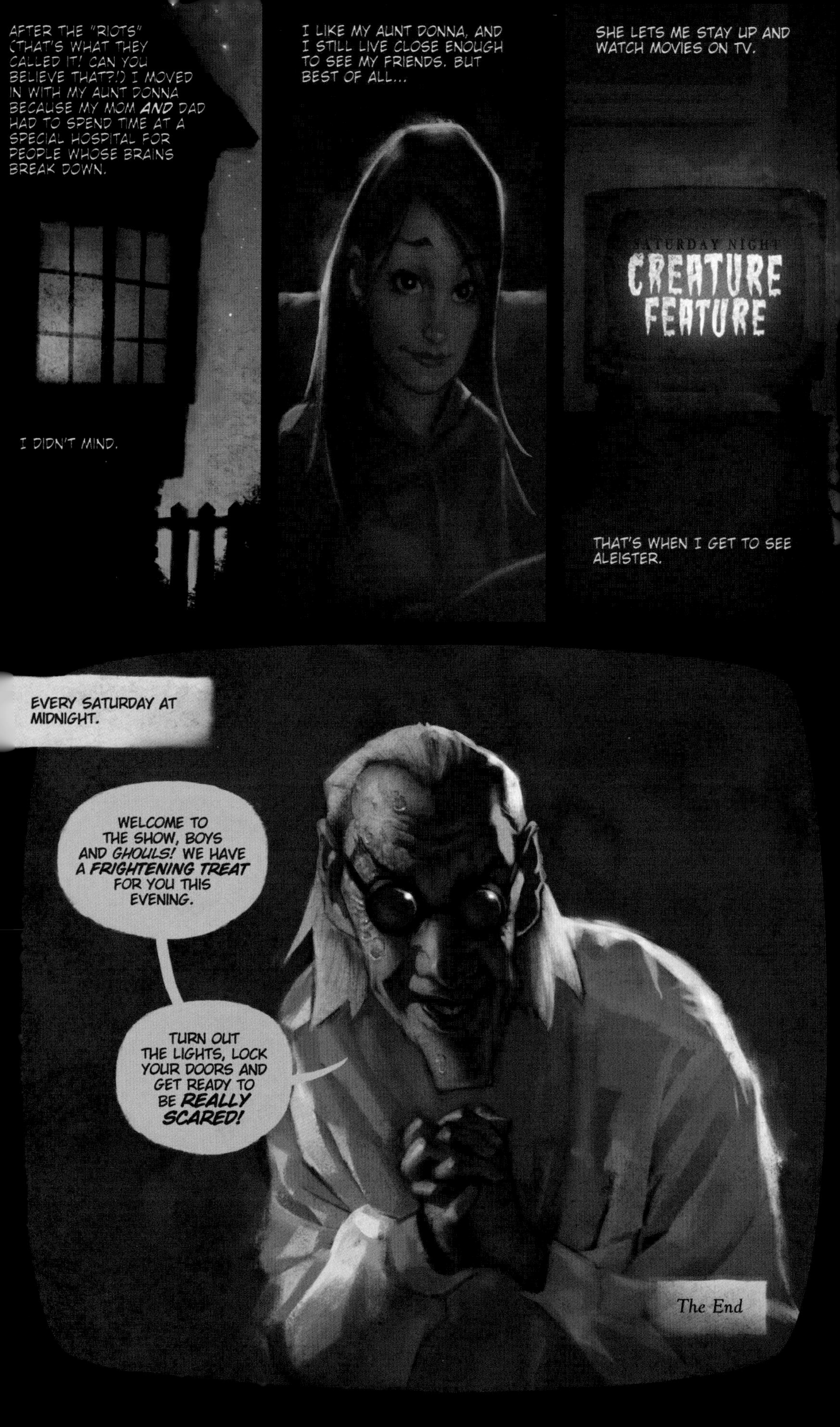
AFTER THE "RIOTS" (THAT'S WHAT THEY CALLED IT! CAN YOU BELIEVE THAT?!) I MOVED IN WITH MY AUNT DONNA BECAUSE MY MOM AND DAD HAD TO SPEND TIME AT A SPECIAL HOSPITAL FOR PEOPLE WHOSE BRAINS BREAK DOWN.
I DIDN'T MIND.
I LIKE MY AUNT DONNA, AND I STILL LIVE CLOSE ENOUGH TO SEE MY FRIENDS. BUT BEST OF ALL...
SHE LETS ME STAY UP AND WATCH MOVIES ON TV.
SATURDAY NIGHT
CREATURE FEATURE
THAT'S WHEN I GET TO SEE ALEISTER.
EVERY SATURDAY AT MIDNIGHT.
WELCOME TO THE SHOW, BOYS AND GHOULS! WE HAVE A FRIGHTENING TREAT FOR YOU THIS EVENING.
TURN OUT THE LIGHTS, LOCK YOUR DOORS AND GET READY TO BE REALLY SCARED!
The End

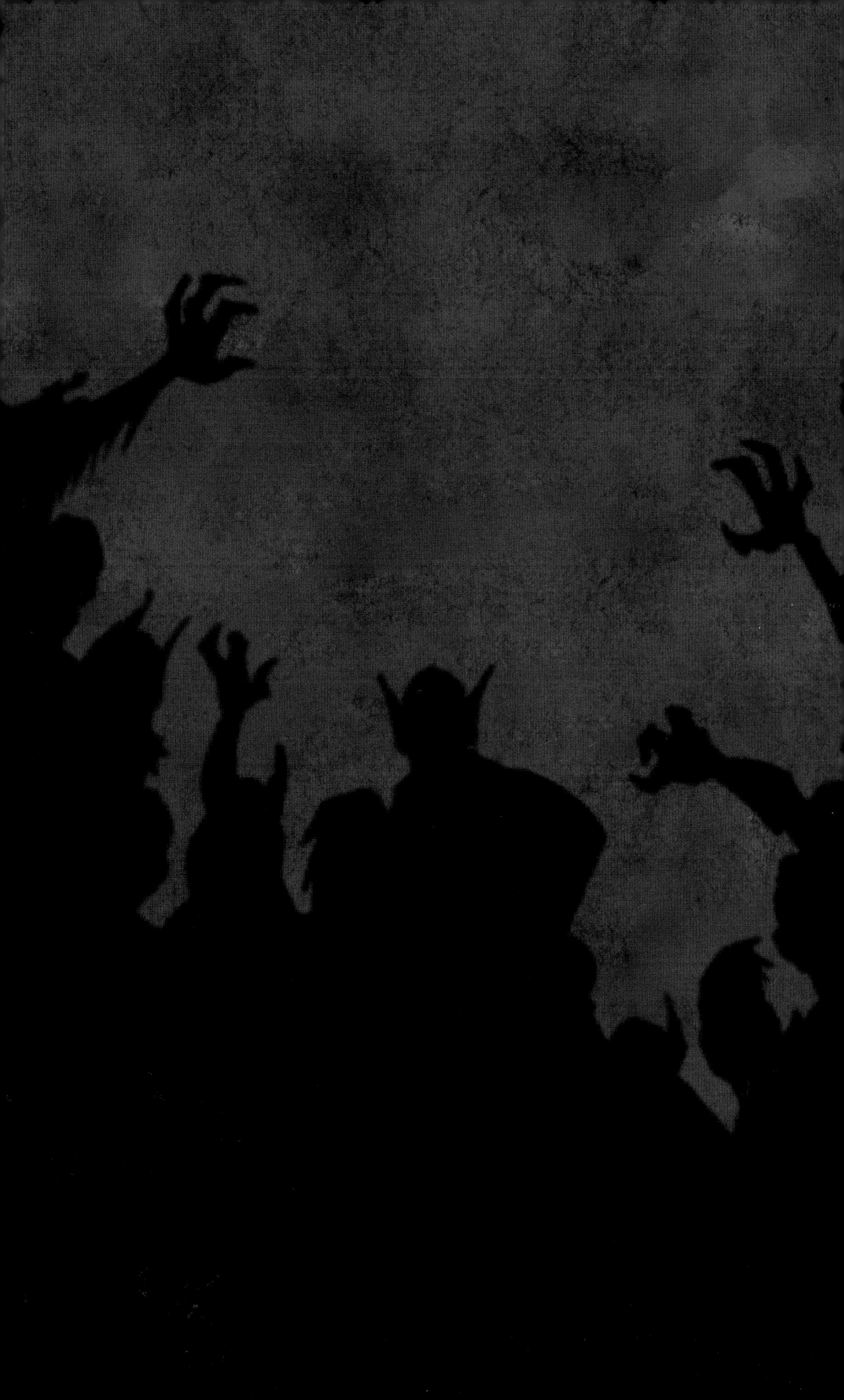

Breehn Burns Sketchbook

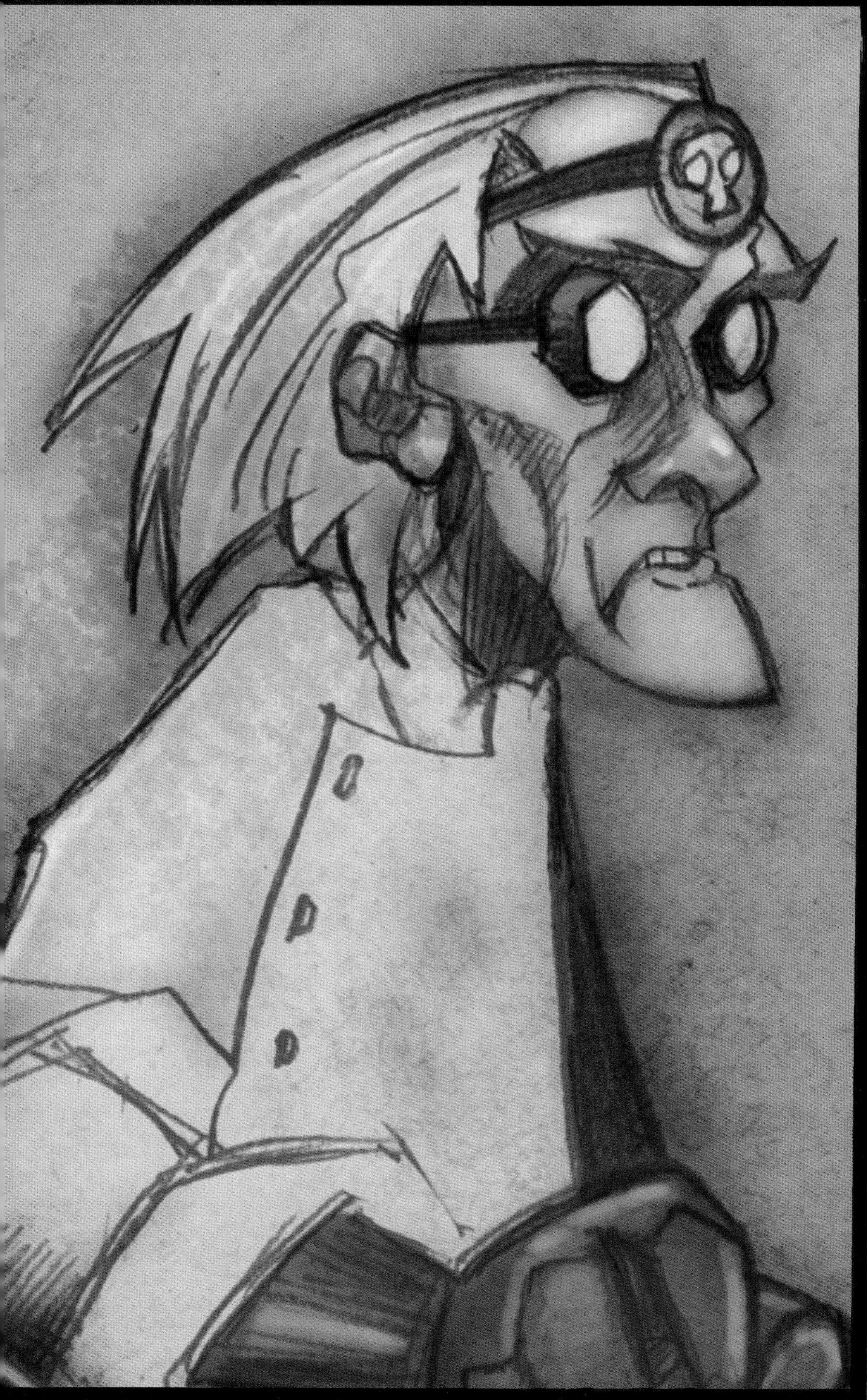

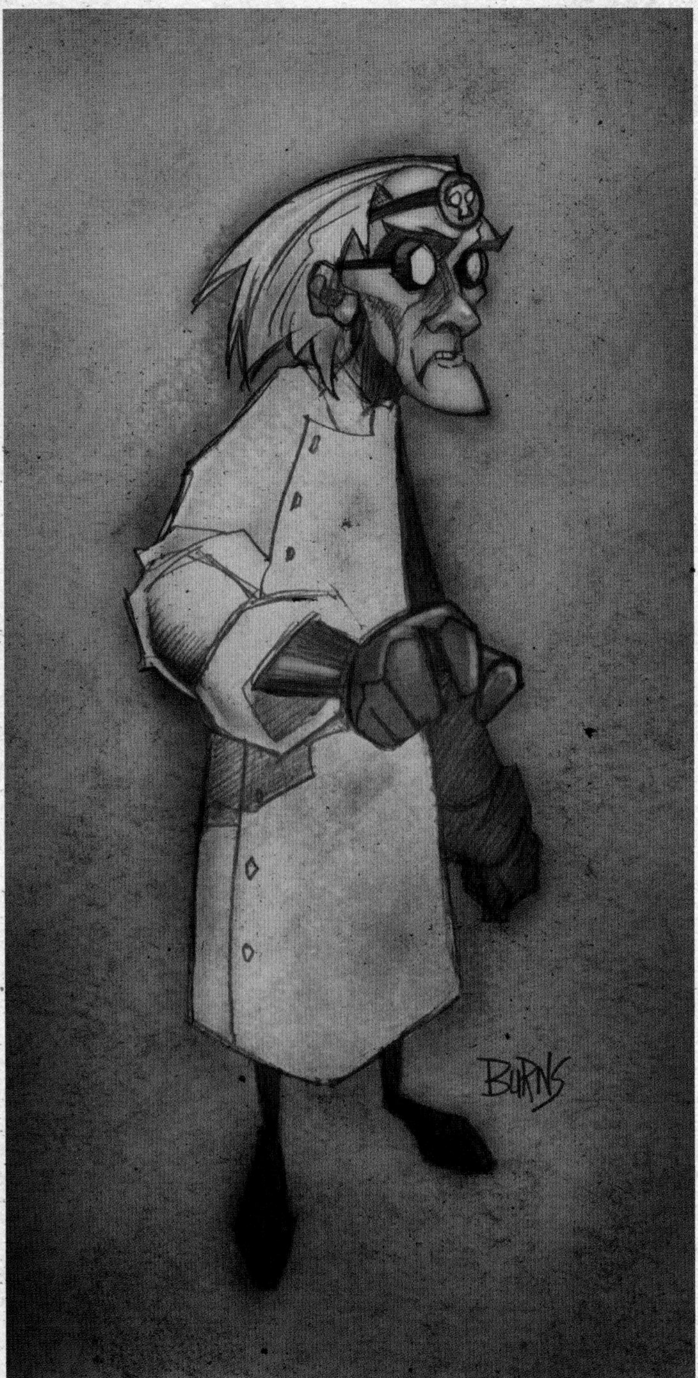
BURNS

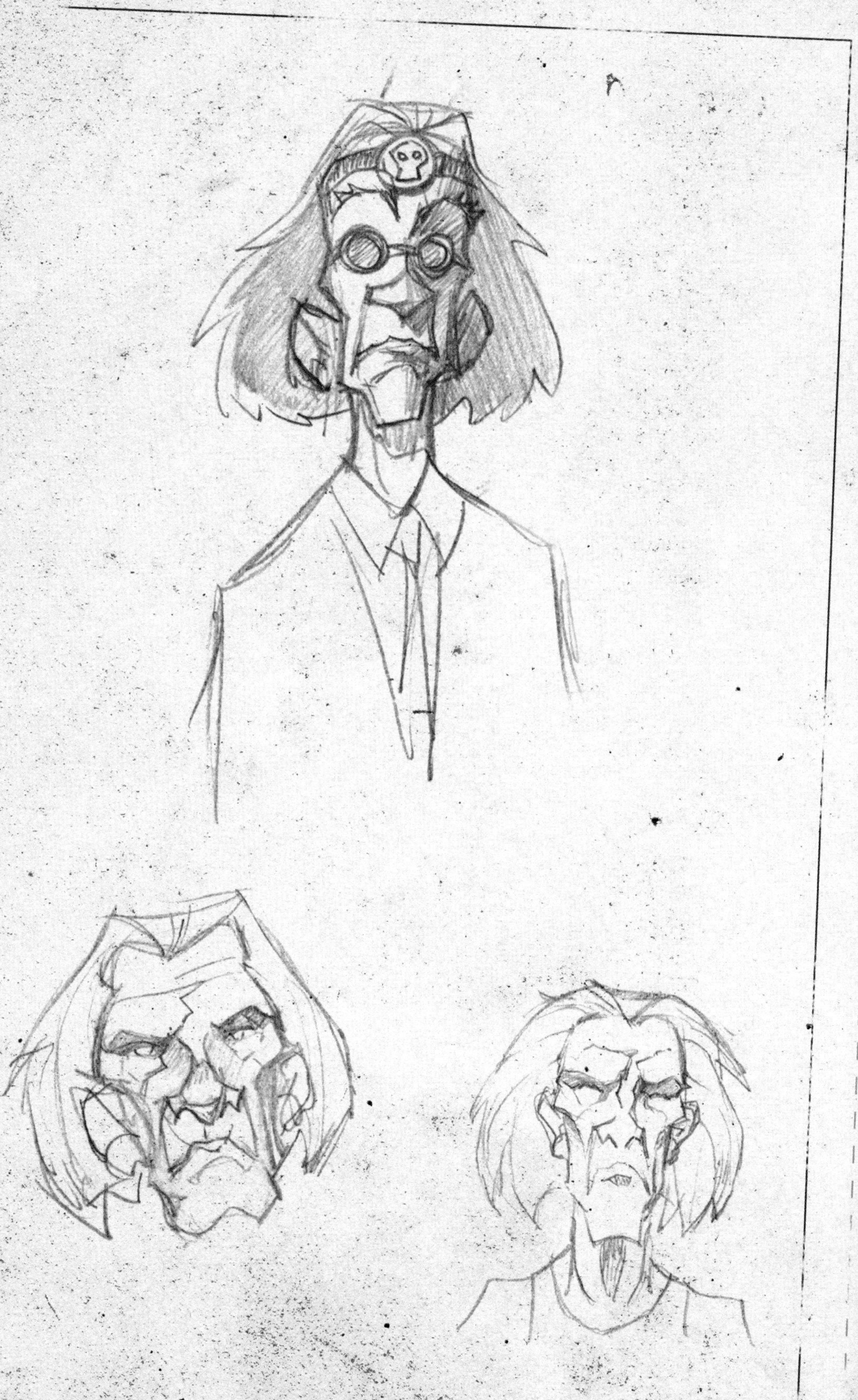

Early Aleister Sketches

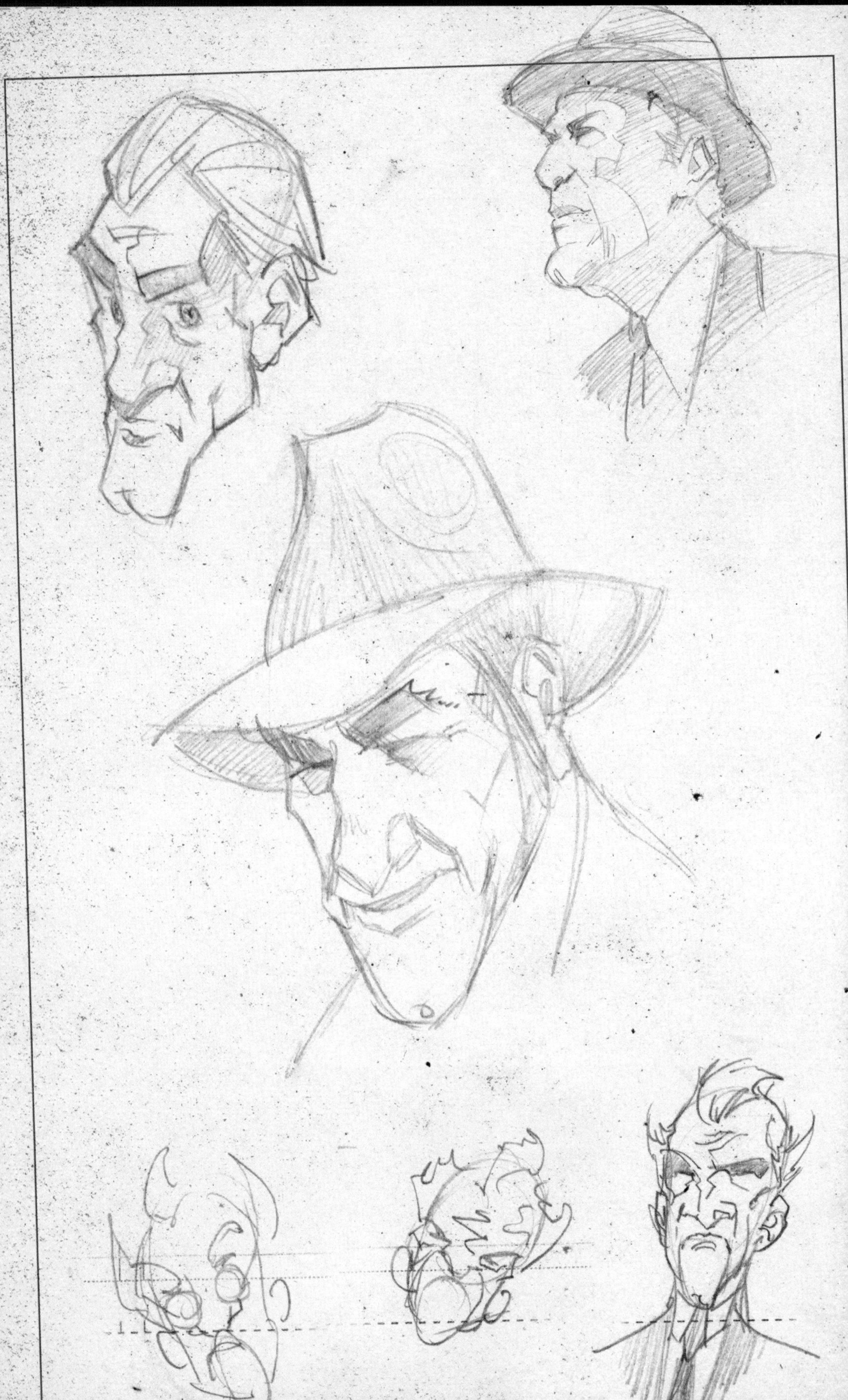

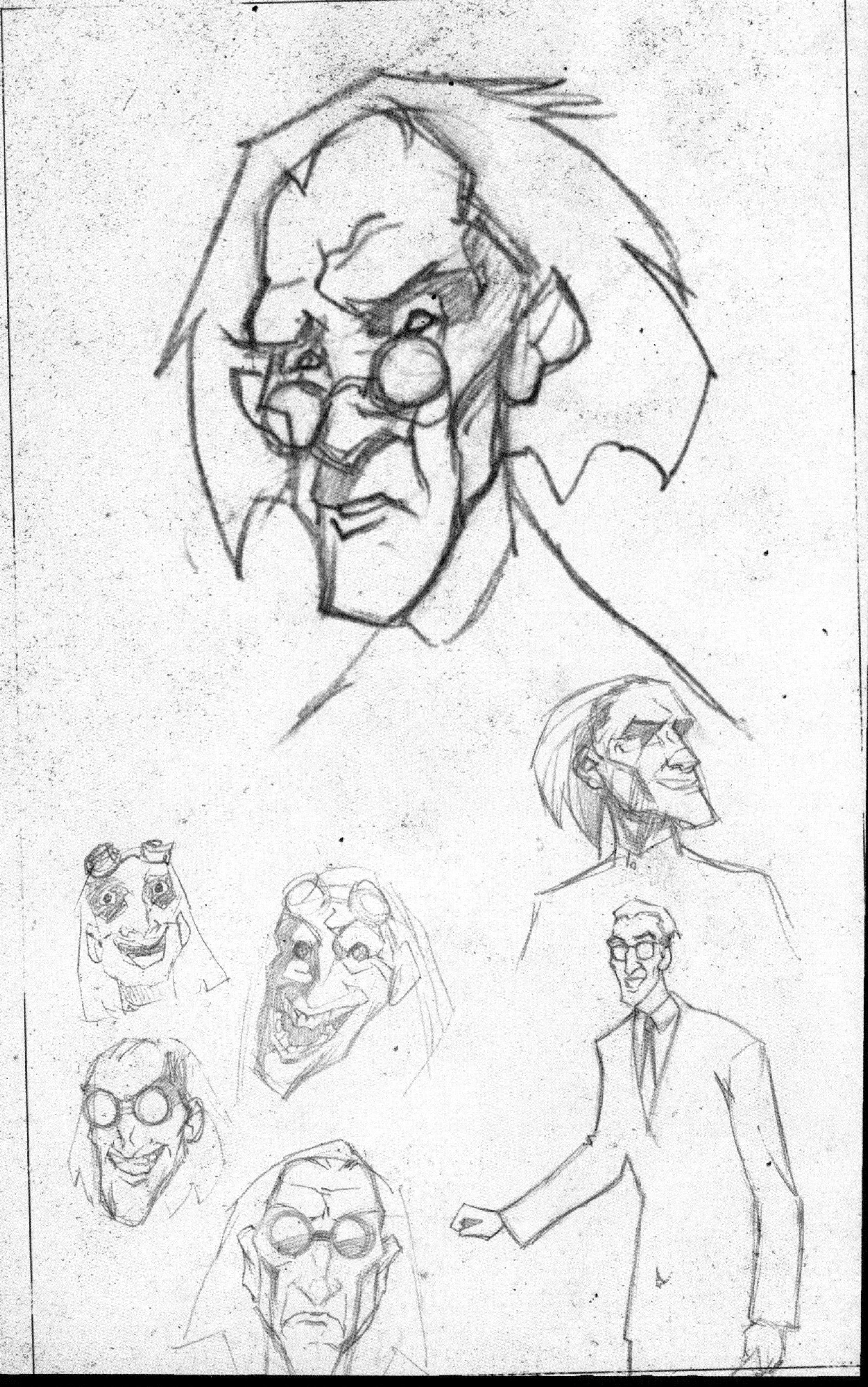

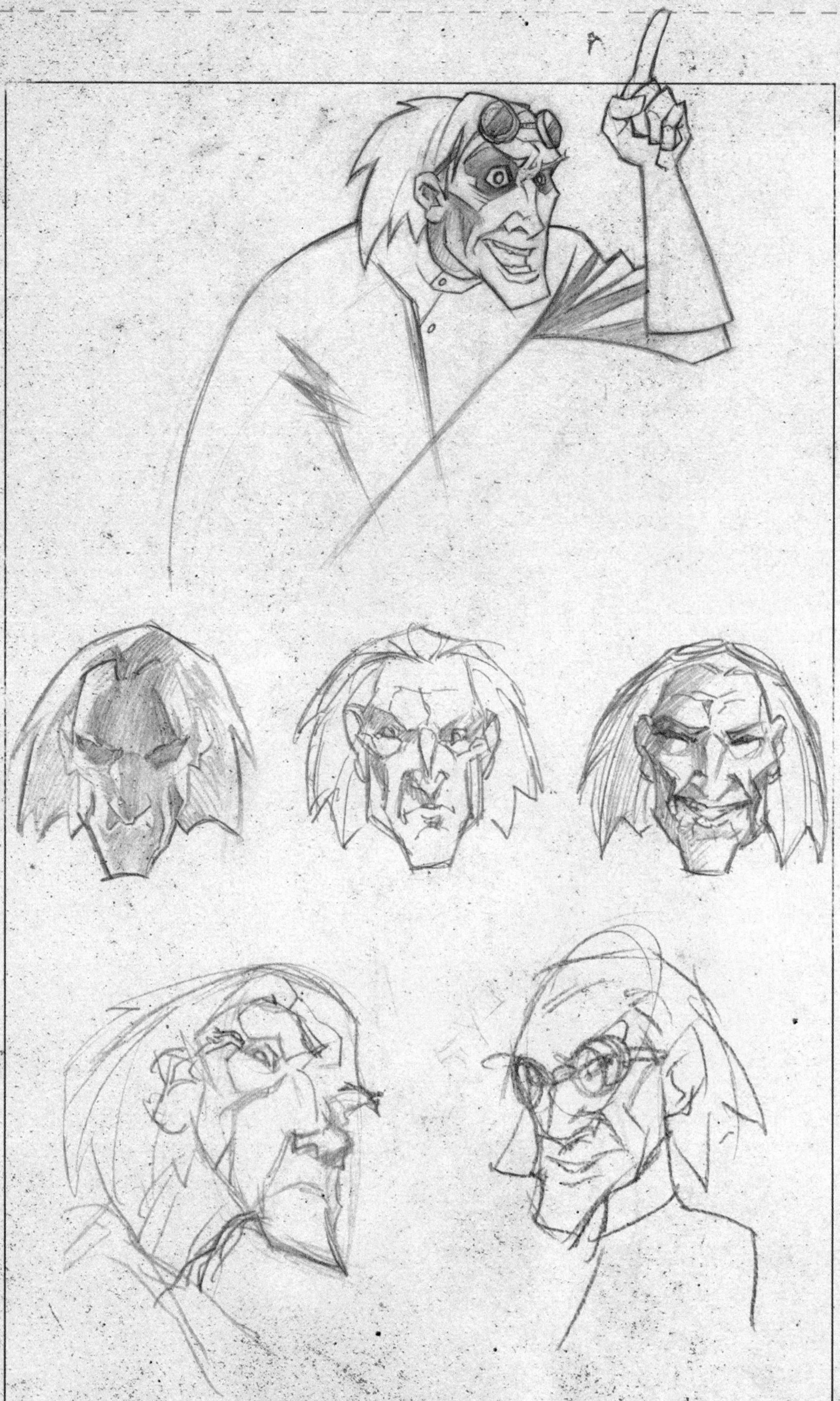

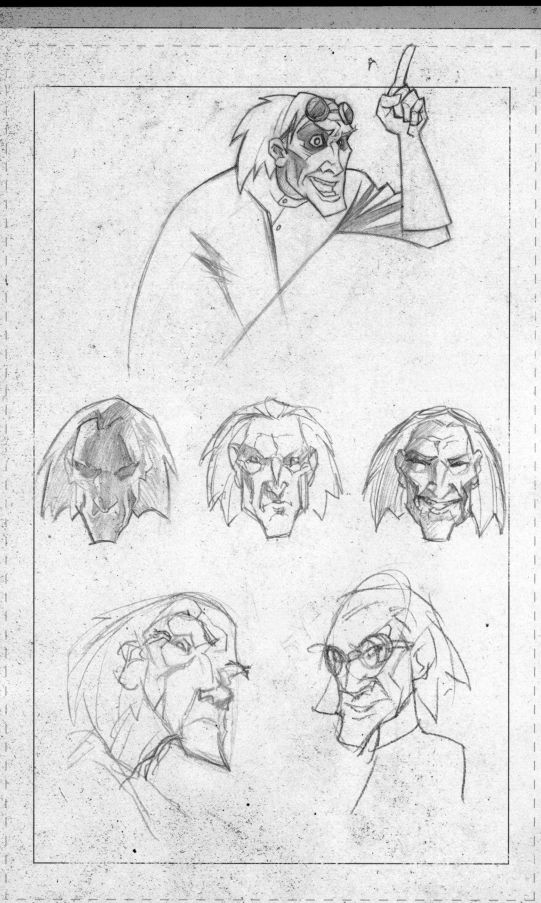

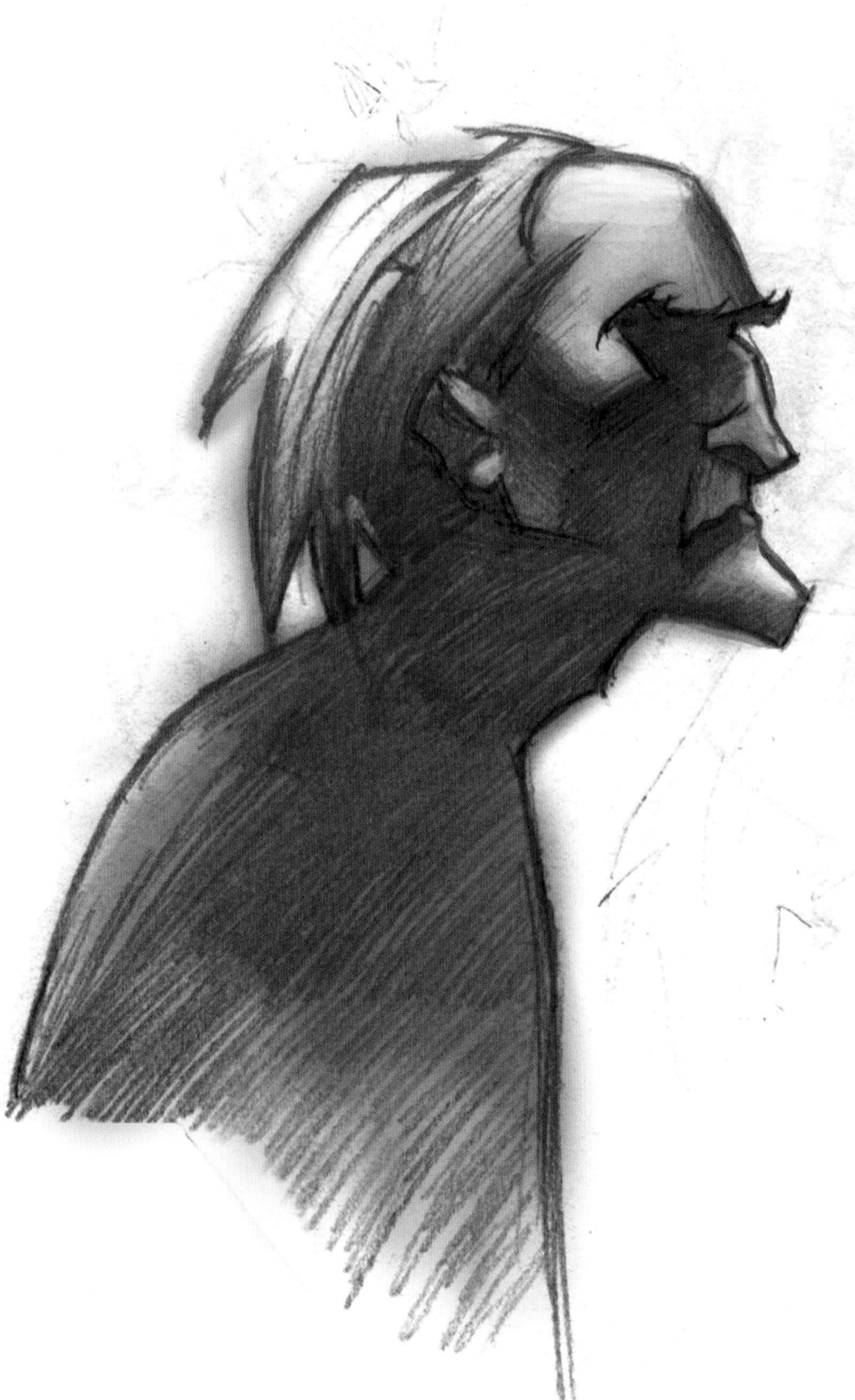

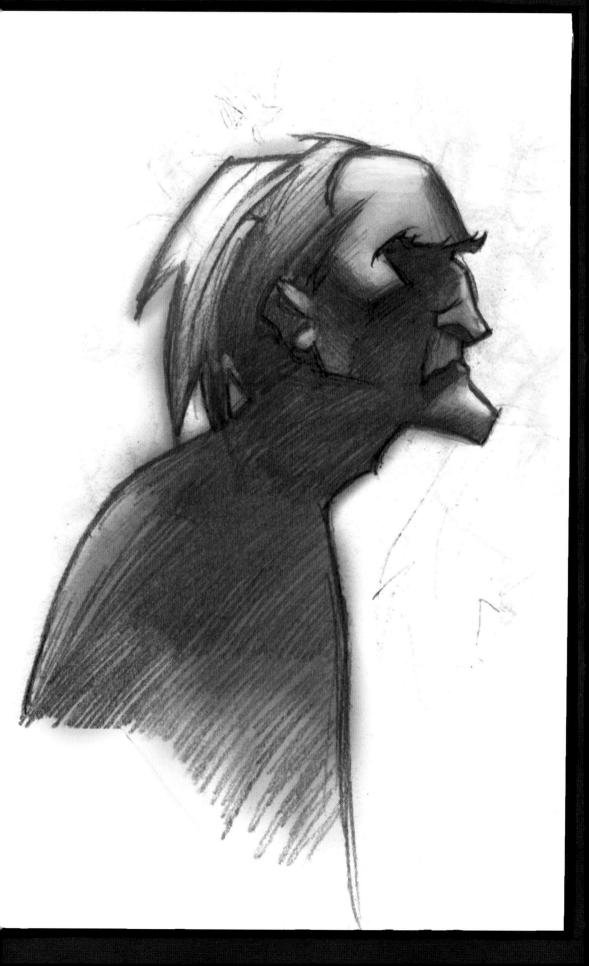

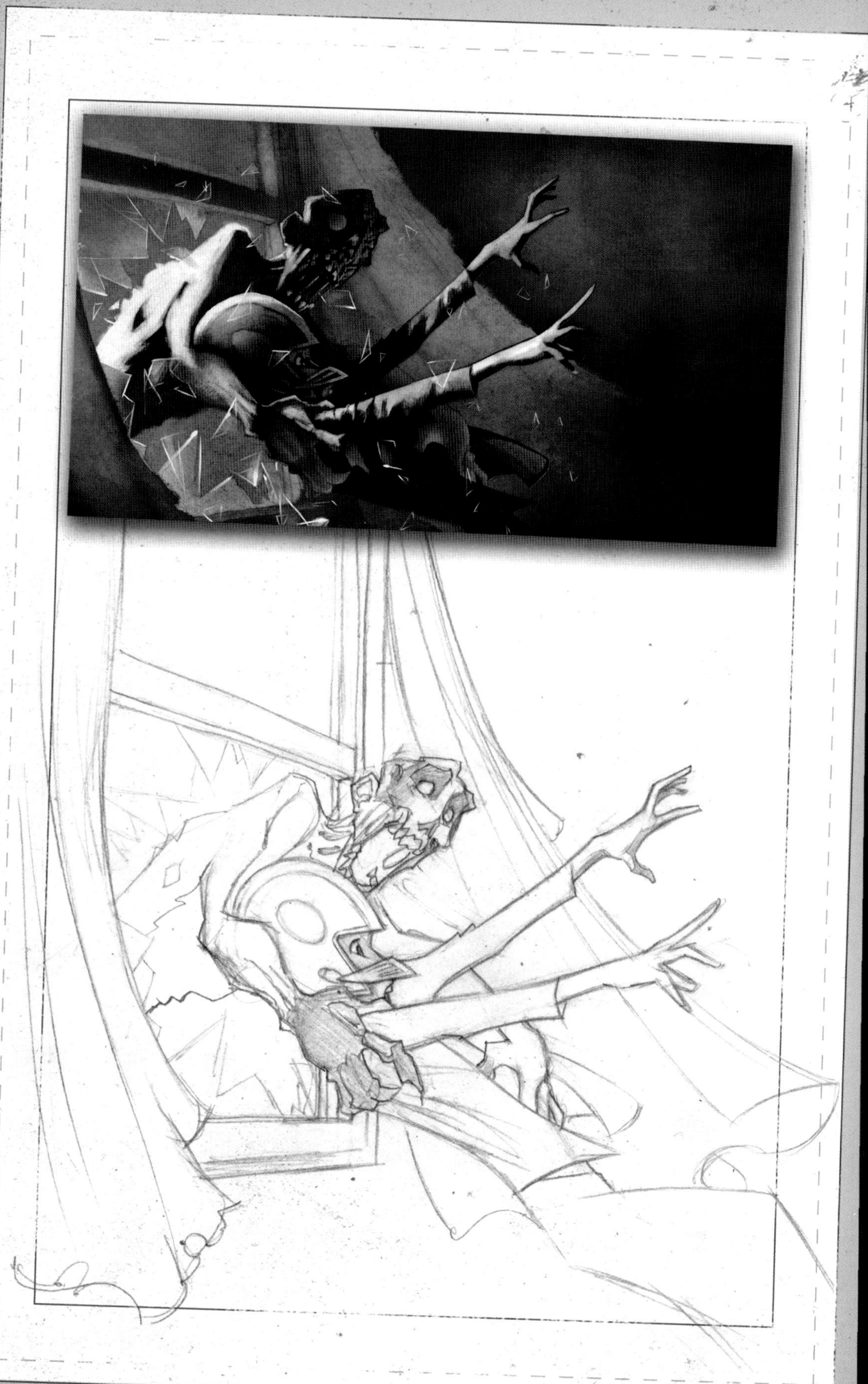

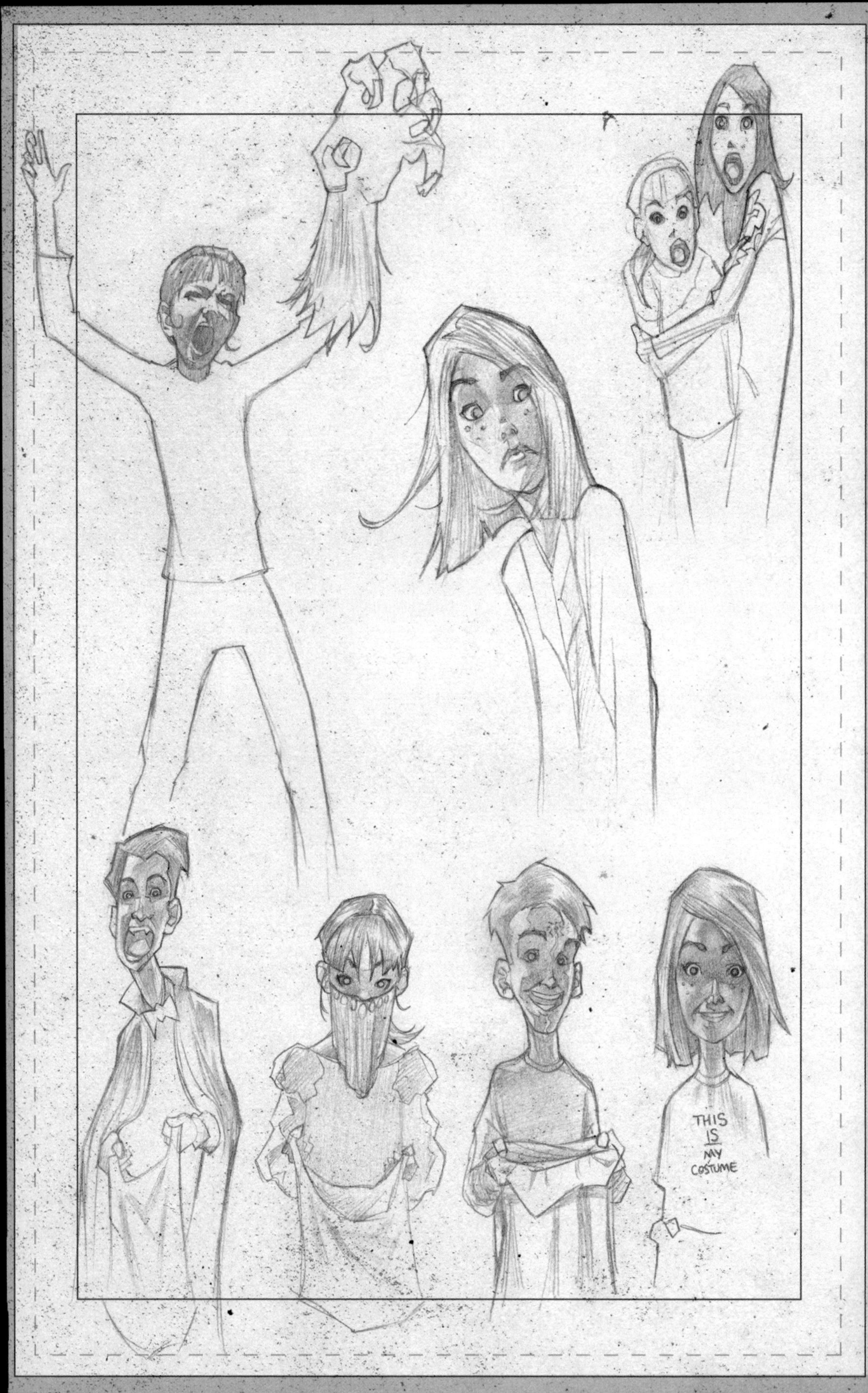
THIS
IS
MY
COSTUME

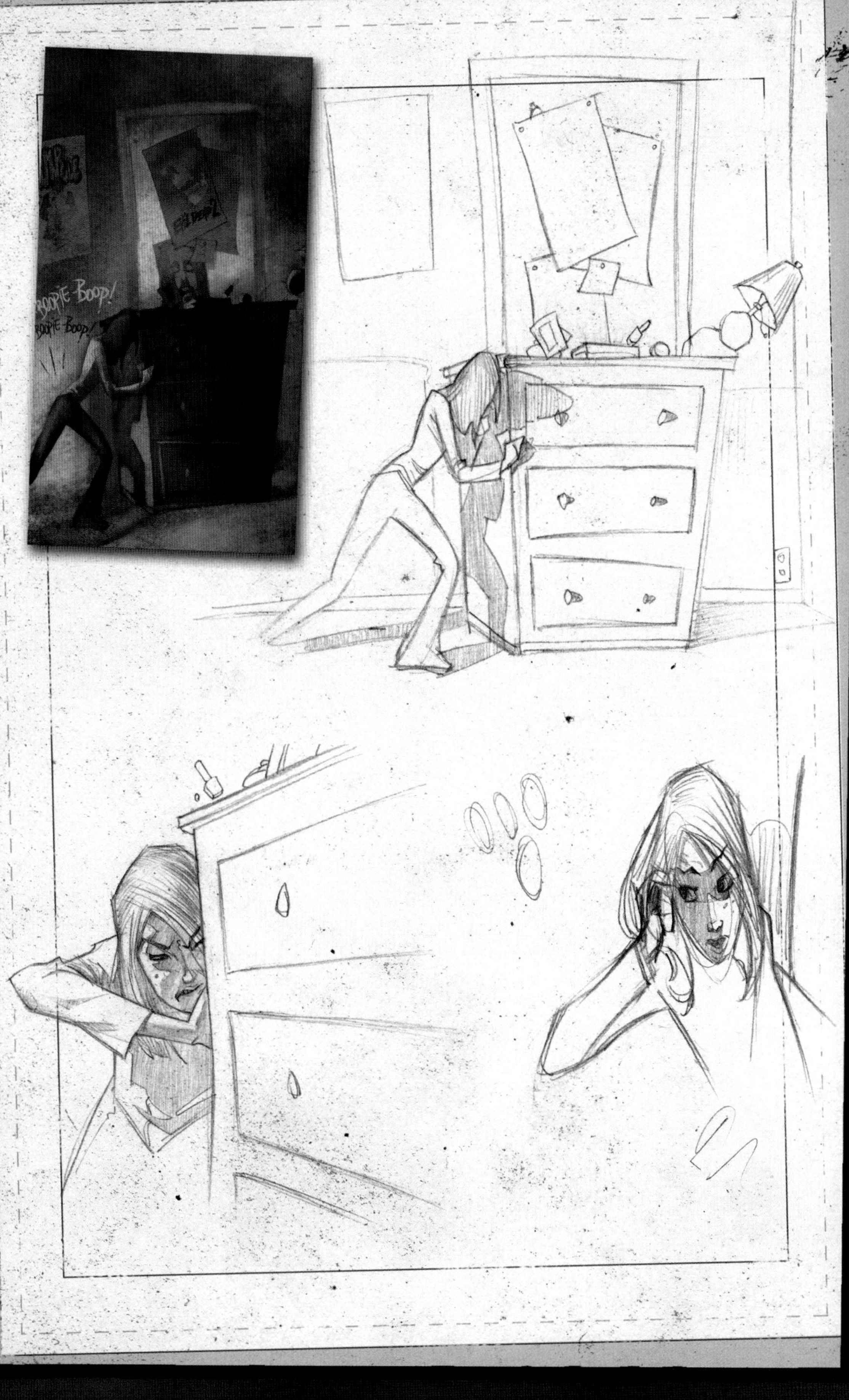

BOOPIE-BOOP!
BOOPIE-BOOP!

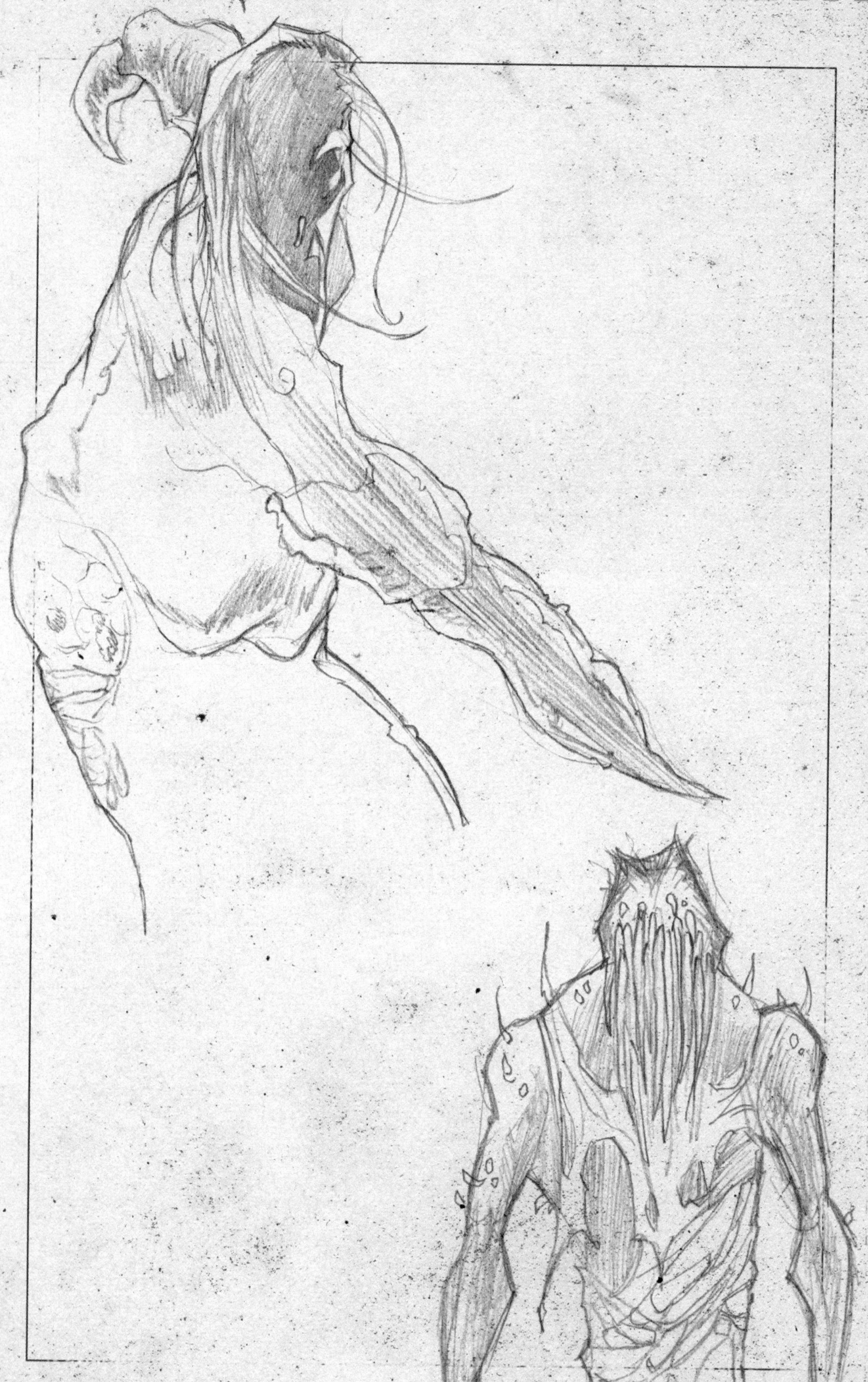

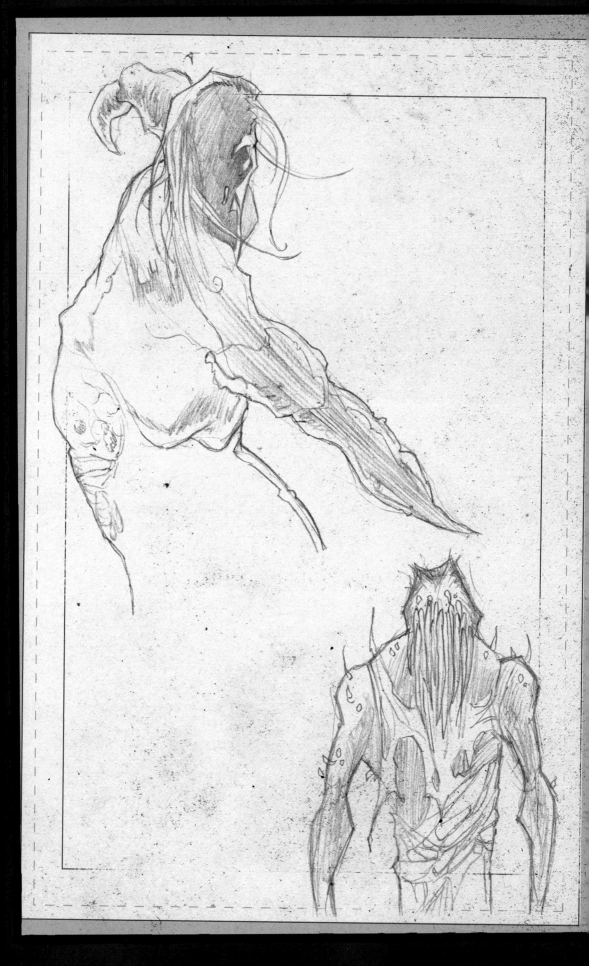

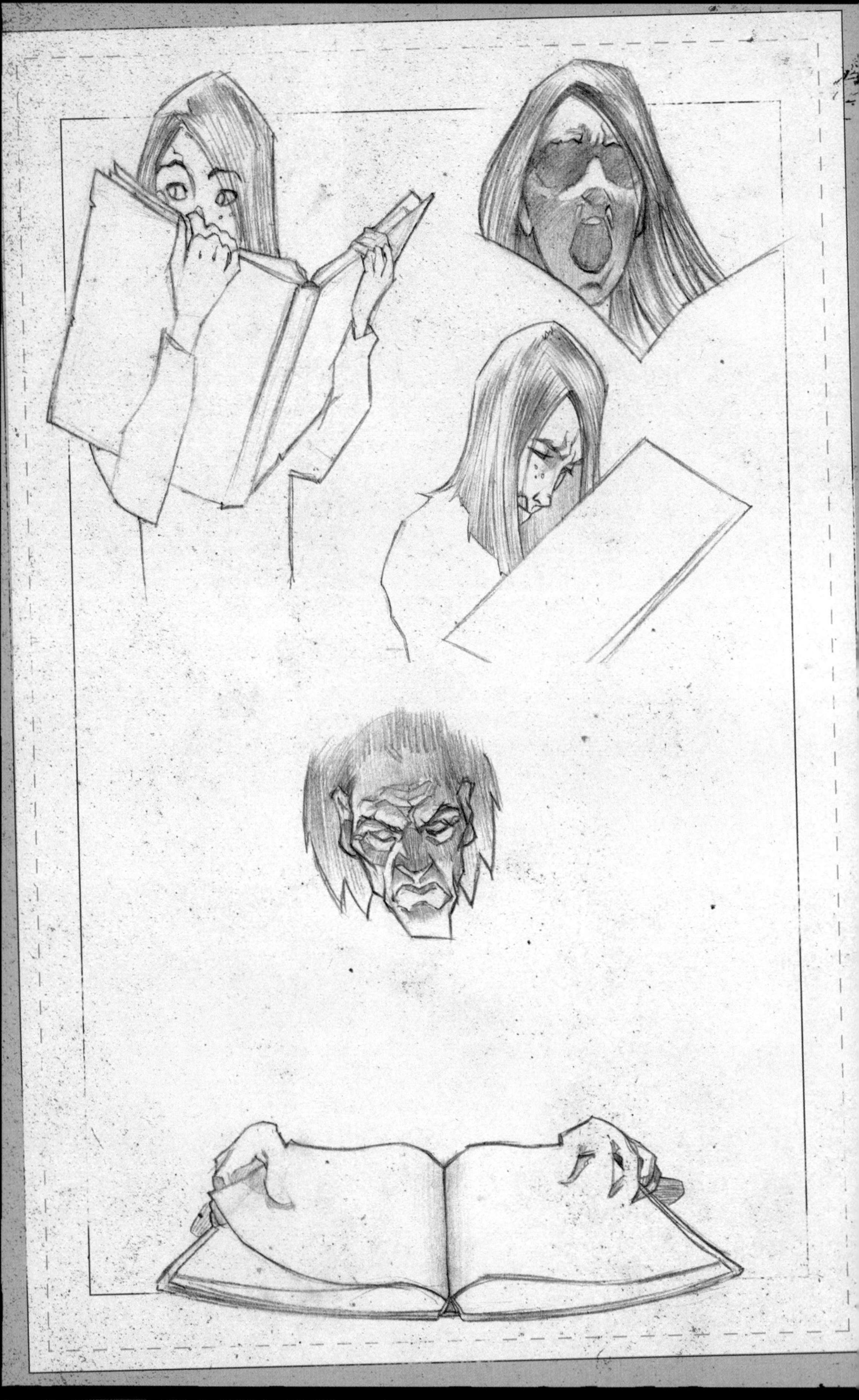

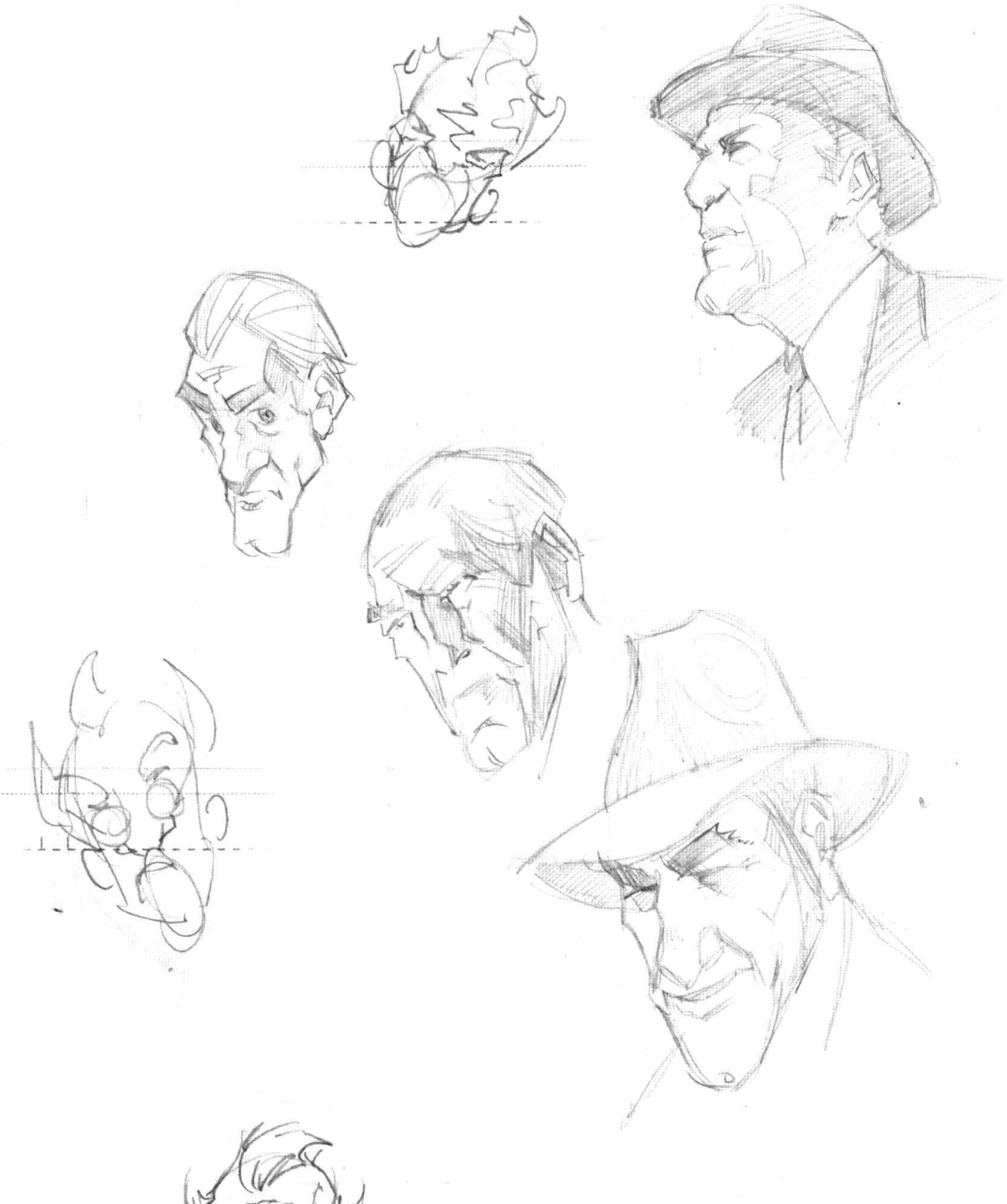

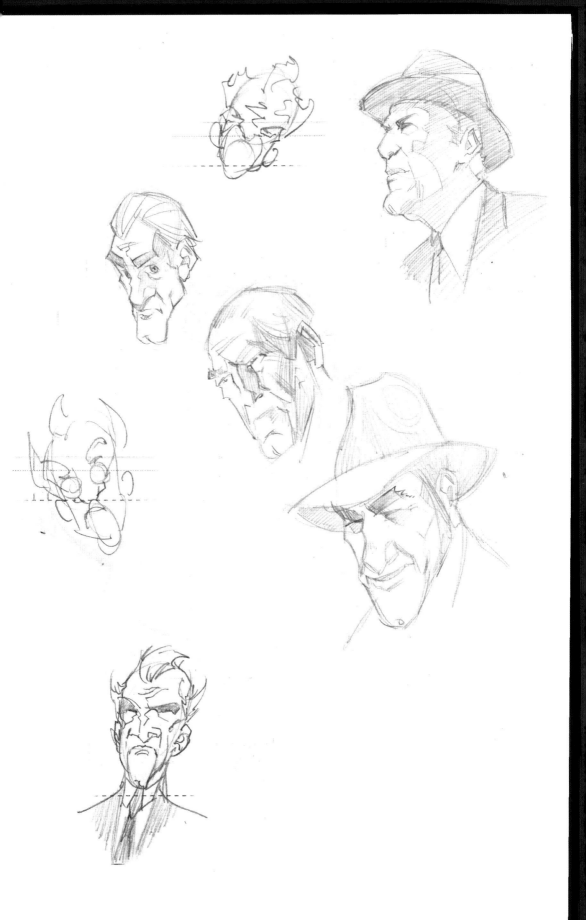

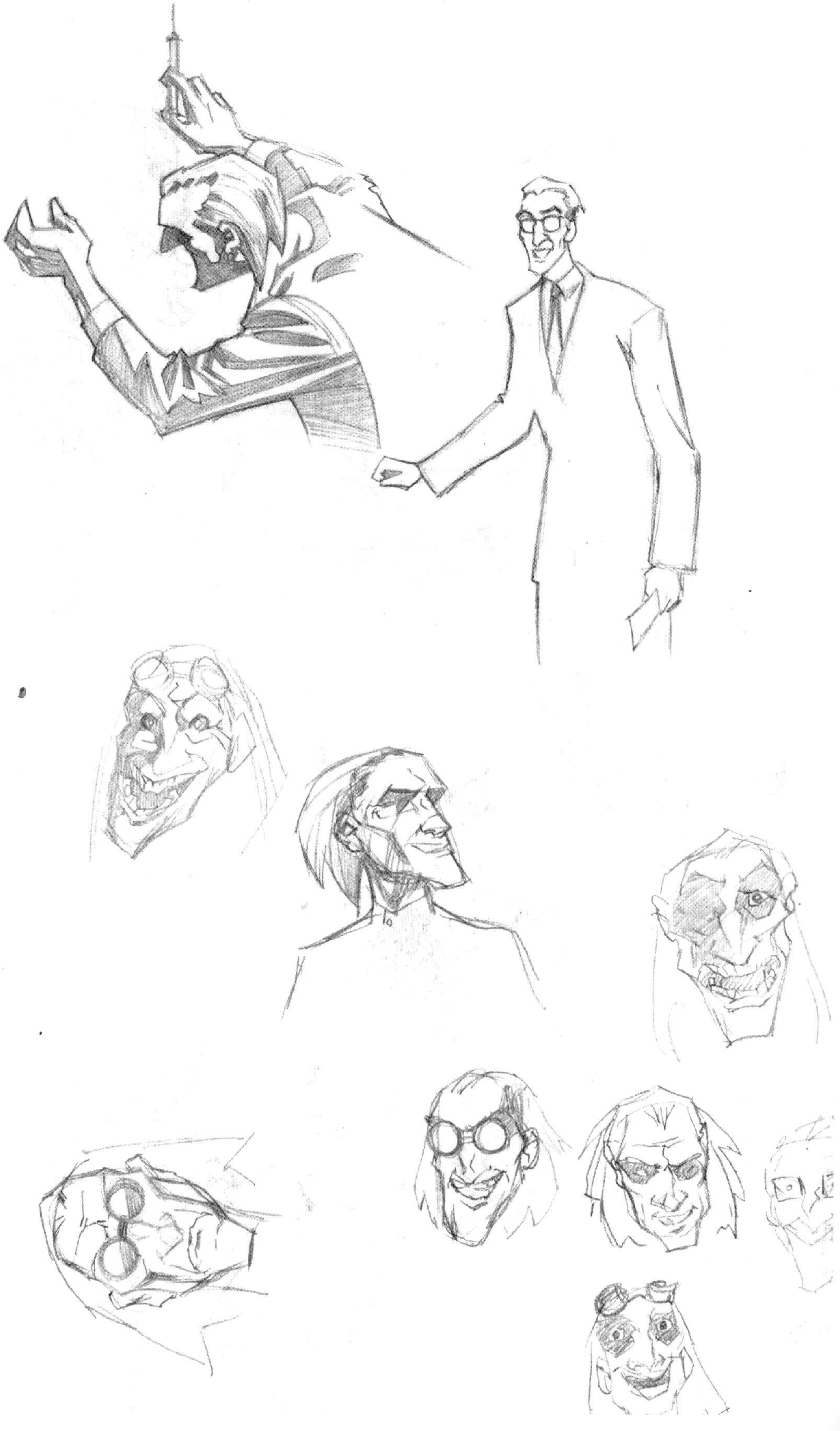

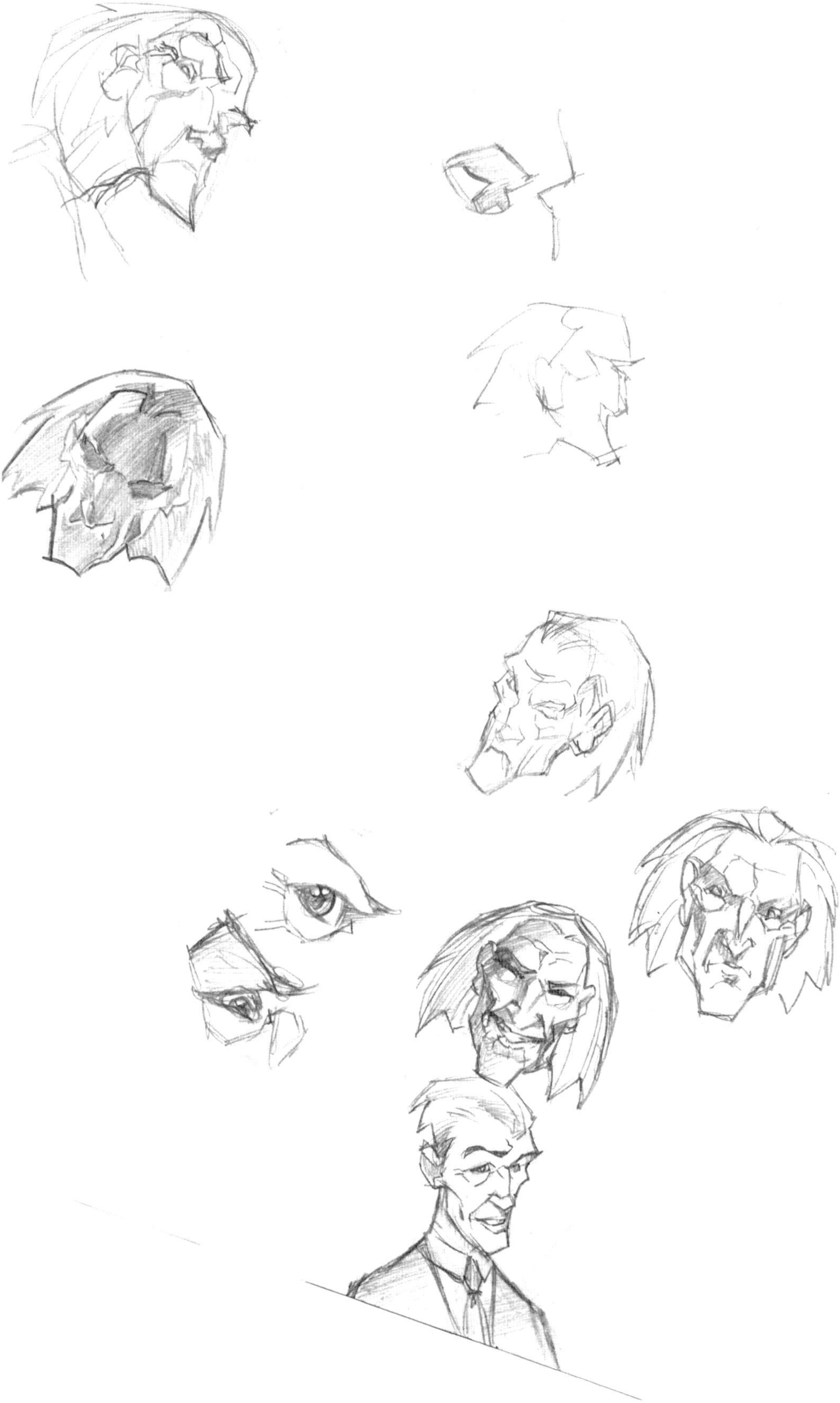

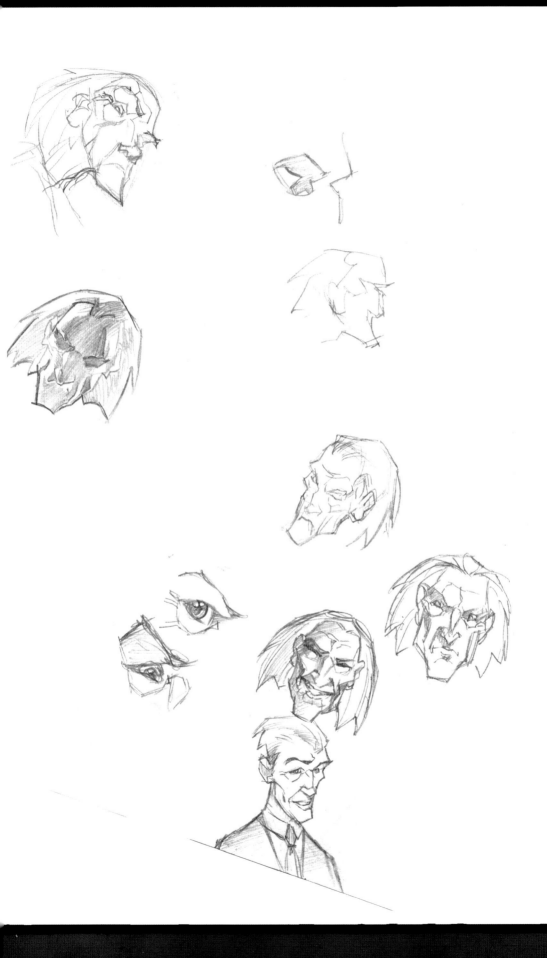

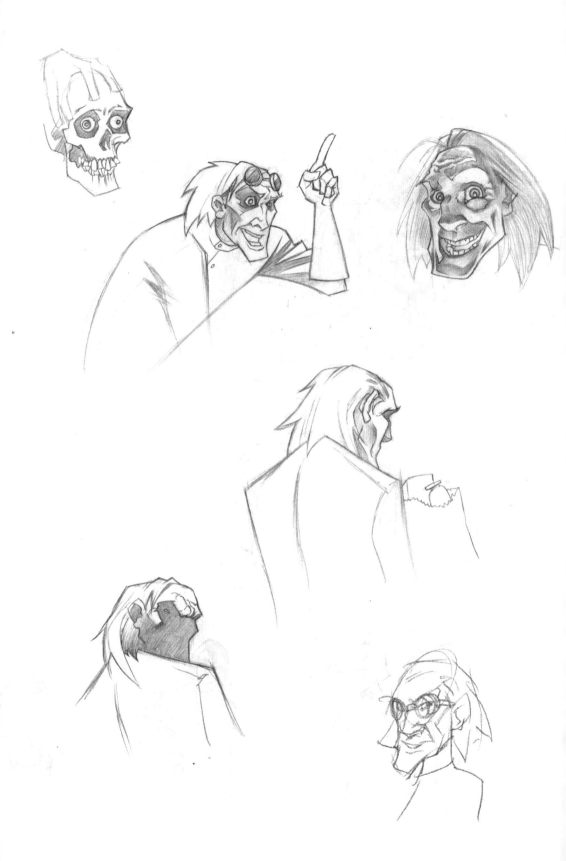

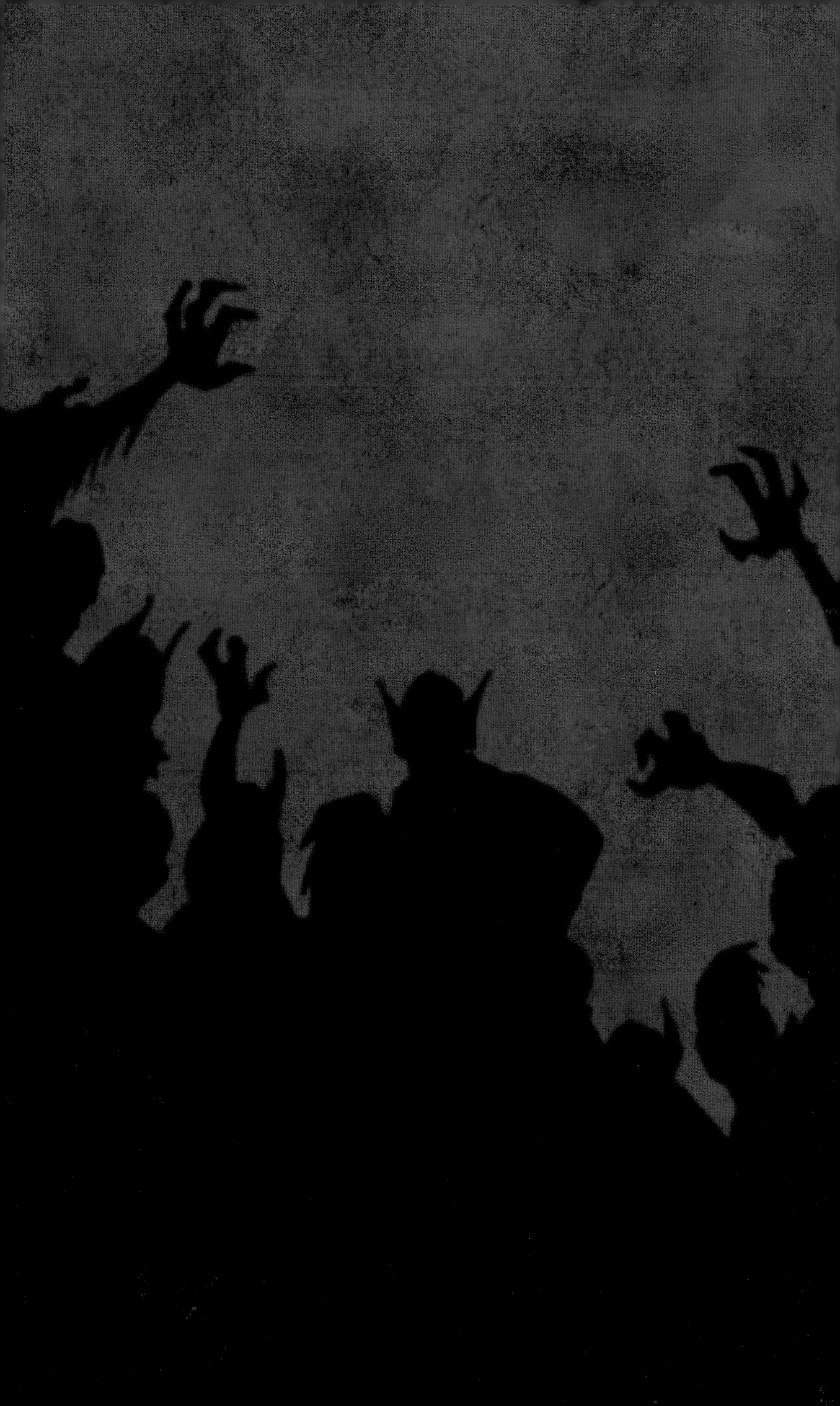

MORE HORROR FROM STEVE NILES

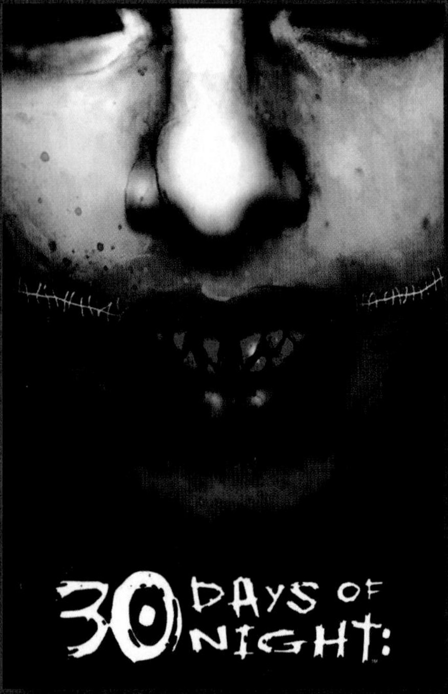
30 DAYS OF NIGHT:

30 Days of Night

ISBN: 978-0-97197-755-6

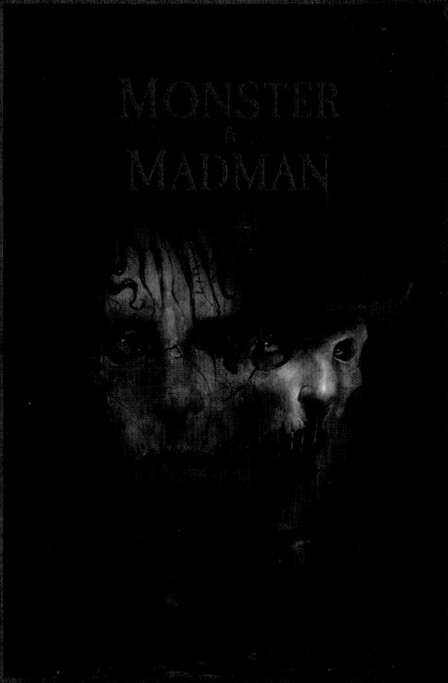
MONSTER & MADMAN

Monster & Madman

ISBN: 978-1-63140-081-0

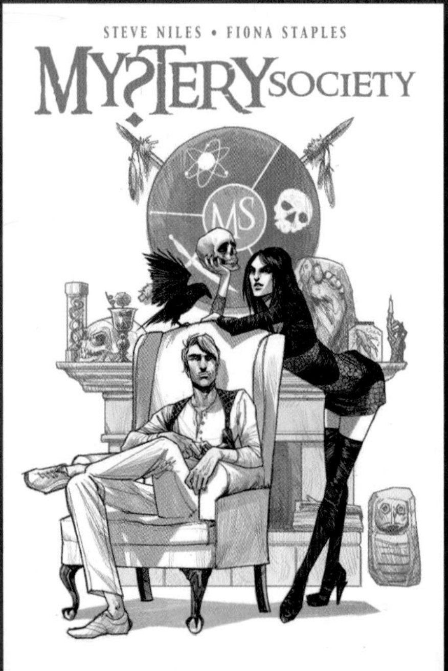
STEVE NILES • FIONA STAPLES
MYSTERY SOCIETY

Mystery Society

ISBN: 978-1-60010-798-6

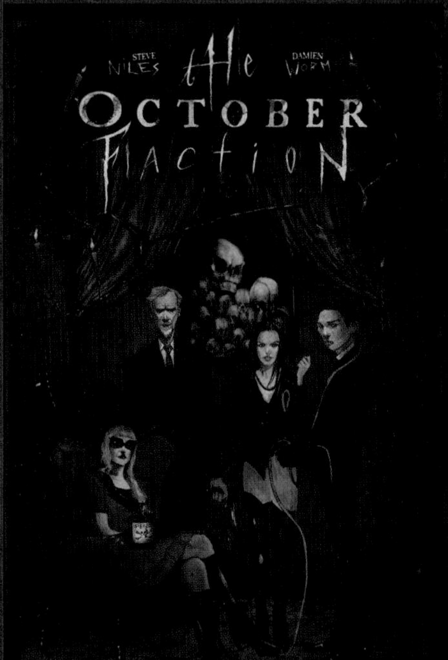
STEVE NILES
DAMIEN WORM
THE OCTOBER FACTION

The October Faction, Vol. 1

ISBN: 978-1-63140-251-7